OSAT®

School Counselor Practice Questions

I0878862

Mometrix
TEST PREPARATION

Dear Future Exam Success Story

First of all, **THANK YOU** for purchasing Mometrix study materials!

Second, congratulations! You are one of the few determined test-takers who are committed to doing whatever it takes to excel on your exam. **You have come to the right place.** We developed these practice tests with one goal in mind: to deliver you the best possible approximation of the questions you will see on test day.

Standardized testing is one of the biggest obstacles on your road to success, which only increases the importance of doing well in the high-pressure, high-stakes environment of test day. Your results on this test could have a significant impact on your future, and these practice tests will give you the repetitions you need to build your familiarity and confidence with the test content and format to help you achieve your full potential on test day.

Your success is our success

We would love to hear from you! If you would like to share the story of your exam success or if you have any questions or comments in regard to our products, please contact us at **800-673-8175** or **support@mometrix.com**.

Thanks again for your business and we wish you continued success!

Sincerely,
The Mometrix Test Preparation Team

Printed in the United States of America

Table of Contents

Practice Test #1 ____ 1
Answer Key and Explanations for Test #1 ____ 16
Practice Test #2 ____ 30
Answer Key and Explanations for Test #2 ____ 46

Practice Test #1

Refer to the following for question 1:

> A counselor currently works in a school with a traditional counseling program that offers crisis counseling in times of need. Additionally, due to a lack of support programs, students who get into fights are often sent to the crisis-counseling program. After witnessing a number of students repeatedly getting into fights, a counselor sees that many fights are due to communication problems and simple misunderstandings, and the school's traditional counseling program is having little effect on students involved in fights. As a result, the counselor decides to change the current counseling model to a developmental counseling program.

1. In terms of the crisis program, what can he do to adapt this program to fit a developmental counseling model?

a. Implement prevention and intervention programs.
b. Discuss developmental issues during the crisis counseling sessions.
c. Include family members in the counseling.
d. Offer crisis counseling to younger students.

2. Which of the following ASCA National Model documents is used to identify and communicate school counseling program priorities to all stakeholders?

a. Annual calendar
b. Annual agreement
c. School data profile
d. Curriculum action plan

3. Solution-focused brief counseling consists of what six steps?

a. Define problem, determine goals, develop intervention, assign strategic tasks, emphasize positive behavior, terminate counseling
b. Define problem, determine goals, develop intervention, revisit goals, develop a second intervention, terminate counseling
c. Conduct psychoanalysis, determine underlying problem, develop group intervention plan, reinforce behavior, assign strategic task, terminate counseling
d. Identify prevention steps, define problem, determine goals, develop intervention, assign strategic task, terminate counseling

4. Which component of a comprehensive school counseling program systematically provides a developmentally appropriate curriculum to all students?

a. Group counseling
b. Classroom guidance
c. Individual counseling
d. Individual student planning

5. Counselors are often responsible for initiating a parent conference by making a phone call or sending a letter home. What should a counselor do in order to avoid an automatic negative reaction from parents?

a. State all the problems their child is having.
b. Speak with a level of equality and openness.
c. State that things at home must change.
d. Suggest that their child seek additional help.

6. What is one strategy a counselor can use to increase job experience and skills that would require community collaboration?

a. Creating an on-the-job training program
b. Finding part-time jobs for students
c. Offering more career-based or skill-improvement courses, such as auto shop and computer applications
d. Offering programs that focus on resume writing and interviewing skills

7. Sophie is a 3rd-grade student who wrote in a class assignment that she wants to be a veterinarian when she grows up. Based on Ginzberg and associates' career development theory, which stage of career development is Sophie in?

a. Informal
b. Fantasy
c. Growth
d. Tentative

8. Which of the following is NOT an appropriate method by which a school counselor would support students with disabilities under IDEA?

a. Providing classroom guidance curriculum to students with special needs as part of the full school program
b. Encouraging a student's parents to participate in a scheduled IEP meeting
c. Writing social-emotional goals for a student's IEP to be addressed through counseling
d. Providing short-term, goal-focused individual counseling as part of a student's IEP

9. Researchers examining teen dating and relationships consider peer influences, personal beliefs, and environmental factors. This is known as:

a. The zone of proximal development
b. The pleasure principle
c. Reciprocal determinism
d. Psychological hedonism

10. Which of the following tests taken by students is an example of an aptitude test?

a. ASVAB
b. End-of-grade test
c. SAT
d. TOEFL

11. A middle school counselor receives a phone call from a case manager at a community agency. The agency provides tutoring and enrichment opportunities for low-income students, and the case manager tells the counselor that they are working with several students at the counselor's school and would like to know how they are progressing academically as a result of their tutoring. Which of the following would be the most appropriate way for the school counselor to work with this agency?

a. Tell the case manager that they will have to ask the students' parents for this information, as FERPA prohibits the counselor from sharing academic information with an outside agency.
b. Provide the students' parents with a release of information form which, once signed, will permit the counselor and case manager to share certain information with each other.
c. Share basic information with the case manager as asked because they represent a stakeholder with a "legitimate educational interest" in the students.
d. Send printed copies of the information with the students to provide to the agency so that they can decide what they would like to share.

12. Which of the following describes a classroom accommodation that is likely to be the most beneficial for a student who has difficulty seeing written content on the board?

a. Preferential seating
b. Extended time
c. Wearing glasses
d. Small group instruction

13. Mr. Hunter, a high school counselor, assembles an advisory council consisting of teachers, parents, students, his building principals, and local community members. He meets with members of this advisory council two times per year to review goals and student outcomes for the counseling program. With which component of the ASCA National Model program does this activity most closely align?

a. Define
b. Manage
c. Deliver
d. Assess

14. Kohlberg proposes a developmental theory in which developmental domain?

a. Psychosexual
b. Vocational
c. Moral
d. Life-style systems

15. Which of the following statements about the potential impact of sexual orientation on student outcomes is NOT true?

a. Students who identify as LGBTQ are more likely to have low grades than their heterosexual peers.
b. Students who identify as LGBTQ are more likely to have higher rates of truancy than their heterosexual peers.
c. Students who identify as LGBTQ are more likely to report concerns about their safety while at school than their heterosexual peers.
d. Students who identify as LGBTQ do not have significant differences in academic outcomes compared to their heterosexual peers.

16. A 2.5-year-old child understands how to say hello, ask for a drink, comment, or answer a question using which aspect of language development?

a. Semantics
b. Phonology
c. Syntax
d. Pragmatics

17. What is the most appropriate group size for an elementary counseling group?

a. Fewer than four students
b. At least four, but no more than six students
c. At least eight, but fewer than ten students
d. Ten students

18. Which of the following is NOT true about most commonly used intelligence tests, such as the Stanford-Binet or Wechsler?

a. Intelligence test scores are measured based on a standard bell curve.
b. The average intelligence score is 100, based on the individual's age group.
c. Intelligence tests are statistically valid and reliable.
d. Intelligence tests are valid across different cultures.

19. Grace is a high school student who asks her school counselor for support in choosing a career path. Using Frank Parsons' career counseling approach, what would be the first step Grace's counselor should take in beginning the career counseling process?

a. Having a conversation with Grace about her goals, interests, aspirations, and personality
b. Having Grace complete several tests in order to collect data about her personal traits
c. Having Grace research careers that interest her to identify possibilities
d. Having Grace complete the Self-Directed Search to determine her personality type

20. Counselors may deny a client's request to view some or all their counseling records only when:

a. There is compelling evidence suggesting that access would cause harm to the client.
b. There is compelling evidence suggesting that the client would require extensive and timely assistance in interpreting the records.
c. The counselor providing services has experienced incapacitation, death, retirement, or has terminated their practice.
d. The situation involves multiple clients, and the requesting client cannot agree to keep the other clients' information confidential.

21. Collaboration with other teachers is a good way to incorporate positive behaviors and communication throughout the school. How can a teacher advisor program assist in this collaboration?

a. It provides all-around support to the students.
b. It makes the teacher feel important and more willing to work with the counselor.
c. It provides more watchful eyes for bad behavior.
d. It gives students more opportunities to get help with their schoolwork.

22. Career counseling based on Bandura's social cognitive theory emphasizes all of these concepts EXCEPT:

a. personal agency.
b. positive uncertainty.
c. self-efficacy.
d. vicarious learning.

Refer to the following for question 23:

A middle school counselor analyzes attendance data and finds that, in a specific classroom, all but six students have attendance rates above 90%. These six students are failing several classes, mostly due to incomplete assignments, missing homework, and late projects. The teacher has contacted the students' parents but has not tried anything else to address these problems.

23. Which of the following interventions would be appropriate in this scenario?

a. Holding a parent information night about grading policies and course requirements
b. Conducting a classroom guidance lesson about how to calculate class averages and the impact of individual assignments
c. Initiating a special education referral for each of the six students to evaluate for executive functioning deficits or learning disabilities
d. Conducting a small group focused on academic skills, such as time management and organizing assignments

Refer to the following for question 24:

Anthony is a 5th-grade student who struggles with focus and attention in the classroom. He has been getting poor grades on assessments and classwork for several months, complaining of headaches, and demonstrating a short attention span in class. His teacher has come to the counselor because she doesn't know how to help Anthony. He does not have a formal diagnosis of ADHD.

24. Which of the following would be an appropriate internal referral for the student described?

a. The school psychologist for a psycho-educational evaluation
b. The school nurse for a vision screening
c. The exceptional children's division for a full evaluation
d. The school social worker for suspicion of abuse or neglect

25. The ASCA Mindsets & Behaviors for Student Success outlines standards or student learning that can be addressed through a classroom guidance curriculum. Which of the four components of the ASCA National Model Program includes these standards?

a. Define
b. Manage
c. Deliver
d. Assess

26. Which of the following is a primary resource for research on school counselor effectiveness?

a. State school counselor associations
b. University counselor education programs
c. ASCA
d. US Department of Education

27. According to Kohlberg's theory of moral development, a student will follow school rules in order to avoid receiving detention. This is an example of what stage of moral development?

a. Personal Reward
b. Law and Order
c. Good Boy-Nice Girl
d. Punishment-Obedience

28. Cognitive behavioral therapy relies on Albert Ellis's ABC model (originally developed as part of rational-emotive behavior therapy). What is the counselor analyzing when using the ABC model?

a. The client's environment
b. The client's emotional state
c. The client's thoughts or beliefs
d. The client's behaviors

29. A recent transfer student came from an inner-city school to your rural school. She is having difficulty adjusting to the area and the school. As the counselor, what steps can you take to ease this student's transition?

a. Announce that there is a new student and ask volunteers to show her around the school.
b. Create a support team with the help of other students, teachers, and the new student's parents.
c. Provide solution-focused brief counseling to the student to find out the underlying problem.
d. Provide information about making friends, and offer this information to the student and her parents.

30. A child is upset with his mother because he believes that his sister received more cookies than he did. The mother gave the siblings the same amount; however, his sister's cookie was broken in half, so she had more pieces of cookie. The brother is in which of Jean Piaget's stages of development?

a. Sensorimotor
b. Preoperational
c. Concrete operational
d. Formal operational

Refer to the following for question 31:

At the beginning of a counseling relationship, the counselor informs the student of confidentiality, stating that he cannot reveal anything that is discussed during the sessions no matter what. After a few sessions, the counselor feels that the student would benefit from extra sessions and offers to meet the student outside of school to talk over coffee. During these after-school sessions, the student informs the counselor that she is considering suicide. Since the counselor does not think this student will follow through, he disregards the statement.

31. What ethical consideration did this counselor violate with the sessions outside of school?

a. Professional Competence
b. Dual Relationship
c. Appropriate Referrals
d. Confidentiality

32. Counselors leading group counseling sessions for students have an ethical obligation to obtain informed consent from all group participants. Which of the following is NOT a part of informed consent in a group counseling setting?

a. Limits of confidentiality
b. Parental consent
c. Knowing other group members
d. Purpose and goals of the group

33. A school counselor who recently completed an annual program evaluation is planning how they will share their results. Which of the following methods for sharing program results is least likely to achieve the goals outlined by ASCA for sharing results?

a. Printing a hard copy of the results report to keep in the counseling office
b. Presenting the results report to the school board and administration
c. Including the results report on the counseling department website
d. Sharing the results report with the counseling advisory committee

34. A school intervention team is reviewing a functional behavior assessment to create a behavior intervention plan. When the team analyzes the data, which of the following would NOT be a possible function of the behavior?

a. Escape
b. Access
c. Sensory
d. Communication

35. A school counselor is part of a school team tasked with developing an intervention plan for a 7th-grade student with severe social/emotional deficits and behavioral concerns. The team decides that, in order to understand the student's behavior, they must conduct an evaluation of the student's functioning in a variety of settings, including at school, at home with the immediate family, and in the community. The team's approach to evaluation best represents which of the following theories?

a. Bronfenbrenner's ecological systems theory
b. Bowen's family systems theory
c. Vygotsky's social development theory
d. Piaget's cognitive development theory

36. A school counselor is conducting a small group focused on developing social skills. During a group session, a student begins discussing the misbehaviors of another classmate who is not in the group, making many comments about the student's lack of social skills. Which technique would be appropriate to use in response to these comments?

a. Clarification
b. Blocking
c. Linking
d. Active listening

37. Which of the following is an example of a technique specifically used in solution-focused brief counseling?

a. Scaling questions
b. Free association
c. Changing self-talk
d. Empty chair

38. Which of the following questions is answered by the school counseling program evaluation?

a. "How are students different as a result of the school counseling program?"
b. "What measurable progress have students made toward counseling program objectives?"
c. "How effective is the school counseling program in achieving its stated goals?"
d. "What impact has the school counseling program had on academic achievement?"

Refer to the following for question 39:

A teacher approaches a school counselor complaining that her students tend to get into fights because of racial tensions. These fights typically begin with students yelling racial slurs at each other and often end up with one or more of the students being sent to the office because of violence or the threat of violence.

39. How might the implementation of human relations training be beneficial in this class?

a. This type of training teaches anger management techniques.
b. This type of training teaches students how to be friends.
c. This type of training promotes conflict resolution.
d. This type of training promotes an understanding of cultural differences.

40. Which of the following is the correct sequence of stages in Piaget's Theory of Cognitive Development?

a. preoperational, sensorimotor, formal operational, concrete operational
b. preoperational, sensorimotor, concrete operational, formal operational
c. sensorimotor, preoperational, formal operational, concrete operational
d. sensorimotor, preoperational, concrete operational, formal operational

41. What type of skills will a counselor focus on if he wants to increase students' ability to think out problems and find positive solutions to such problems?

a. Basic academic skills
b. Relating skills
c. Conflict resolution skills
d. Cognitive literacy skills

42. Which of the following is an appropriate use of intelligence assessments, such as the WISC, in a school setting?

a. As a component of a psycho-educational evaluation
b. As the sole determinant of eligibility for special education services
c. To guide students toward appropriate career paths
d. To make placement decisions for honors coursework

43. A counselor in a predominately white school does not feel that cultural diversity programs are important in the school. What is wrong with this belief?

a. Non-white students may feel left out of school activities.
b. White students might feel left out of school activities.
c. Cultural diversity involves more than just the color of one's skin.
d. A student may want to attend a college that is very diverse.

44. A school counselor is evaluating end-of-grade assessments for 3rd grade reading at their school. The mean of the scores is 50. What does a mean of 50 represent?

a. The average test score is 50.
b. The highest test score is 50.
c. The most common test score is 50.
d. The percentage of students who passed the test is 50.

45. A client may utilize the ego defense mechanism of *sublimation* in order to do which of the following?

a. Voluntarily block unpleasant emotions
b. Negate an intolerable experience
c. Retreat to an earlier stage of development
d. Redirect socially unacceptable impulses

46. Mrs. Simon is in her second session of individual counseling with a student who wishes to improve her grades. In their first session, the student identified her goal as completing her homework each night and turning it in each day without skipping any assignments; previously, the student had a very poor homework completion rate. Based on solution-focused brief counseling theory, which of the following would Mrs. Simon use to begin their second session?

a. Asking the student what challenges she faced in meeting her goal over the last week
b. Asking the student what is going better since they met last week
c. Asking the student what she was thinking as she completed her homework each night
d. Printing off the student's online grade book and highlighting missing assignments

47. At which stage of the group counseling process does the counselor begin to prepare group members for the termination stage of the group?

a. Selection/screening
b. Initial/forming
c. Transition/storming
d. Working/norming

48. Holland believed that a specific career will tend to attract people with similar personality types. One example would be the occupation of "teacher," which best aligns with which personality type?

a. Artistic
b. Conventional
c. Investigative
d. Social

49. Which of the following is NOT an appropriate strategy for facilitating course selections for middle-school students?

a. Calling a grade-level meeting to discuss course options and having all students fill out a course selection form individually
b. Holding individual meetings with students and their parents to discuss their course options and make selections
c. Incorporating course selections into a classroom guidance lesson and having students fill out a course selection form during the lesson
d. Using grades and standardized test data to assign students to courses based on current achievement

50. Mr. Scott is a new school counselor and is starting to collect data to plan his comprehensive school counseling program. Which of the following is a type of perception data that could be used to plan a new comprehensive school counseling program?

a. School data profile
b. Needs assessment
c. Pre-test data
d. Achievement testing data

51. Which of the following student differences would NOT be a likely cause of cultural bias on a test?

a. Differences in English proficiency
b. Differences in socioeconomic status
c. Differences in classroom grouping
d. Differences in gender

52. Compared to middle school or high school counselors, elementary school counselors must have an especially strong understanding of what?

a. Child development
b. Continued education options
c. Relationship building
d. Adjustment and coping mechanisms

53. When a diagnostic assessment for learning needs is conducted, what factor is NOT considered?

a. Prior knowledge
b. Interests
c. Learning style preferences
d. Sociability

54. Kelly is a second-grade student who demonstrates distractibility, forgetfulness, and task avoidance at school. He struggles to complete tasks, organize his materials, and frequently loses items needed for school. His parents report similar struggles at home. Which of the following disorders could Kelly's symptoms be consistent with?

a. Specific learning disability
b. Autism spectrum disorder
c. Generalized anxiety disorder
d. Attention-deficit hyperactivity disorder

55. The James-Lange theory of arousal and emotion says that:

a. a physiological response precedes emotion.
b. emotion precedes a physiological response.
c. emotion and physiological response occur together.
d. physiological response and emotion are not related.

56. According to Linda Gottfredson, young children around age 6 tend to choose occupations based upon:

a. their social values.
b. their ability levels.
c. their sex or gender.
d. their personal traits.

57. Amy, a high school student, is in crisis. The school counselor is called because Amy is crying uncontrollably in the hallway, making statements about wanting to harm herself. Amy seems visibly calmer after talking with the counselor, but she continues to make concerning statements about wanting to kill herself, indicating that she has a firm plan to carry out an attempt to kill herself that weekend. Assuming each possibility is compliant with school and district policies, what is the appropriate next step for the school counselor to take?

a. Contact Amy's parents to pick her up and encourage them to set up an appointment with a therapist.
b. Call Child Protective Services to conduct an investigation and ensure that Amy is safe at home.
c. Call the local mental health urgent care or crisis response unit to conduct a crisis evaluation.
d. Have Amy sign a no-harm contract, promising not to harm herself and outlining steps she should take if she has suicidal thoughts.

Refer to the following for question 58:

> A counselor begins seeing a student who has issues with low self-esteem. This student is of Chinese descent but was adopted by an African American family as a baby. The counselor knows that children begin understanding their cultural identities by the time they are three years old.

58. What responsibility does the counselor have toward the student regarding culture?

a. Provide the student with information on her Chinese heritage and encourage her to embrace it.
b. Suggest she join the Chinese American Club at school.
c. Question her feelings of being of Chinese descent but being raised in an African American home.
d. Respect the student's cultural identity as it is and assist her instead with the problems she brought to the attention of the counselor.

59. A known bully in the school is referred to your office. In addition to providing intervention for his violent behavior, what common issue or risk factor should you take into consideration?

a. Pathology
b. Potential to drop out of school
c. Future self-esteem issues
d. Poor conflict management skills

60. According to the Social Cognitive Theory, to what does the term "perspective taking" refer?

a. Internalizing another person's situation
b. Thinking cognitively about another person's situation
c. Role playing
d. Thinking cognitively about your own situation

61. Which of the following program evaluation activities could NOT be conducted using data pulled from a school's student information system (SIS)?

a. Evaluate individual attendance data after completion of a small group focused on improving attendance.
b. Evaluate enrollment in advanced coursework by student subgroup as part of a closing-the-gap action plan.
c. Evaluate process data regarding the number of parents who participated in an informational meeting.
d. Evaluate discipline outcome data for a group of students who completed an anger management group.

62. In career self-efficacy theory, which of these is NOT one of the three elements that will be influenced by an individual's expectations?

a. Choice
b. Competence
c. Performance
d. Persistence

63. Carl Rogers' person-centered therapy identifies three key factors necessary for an effective helping relationship. Which of the following is NOT one of these key factors?

a. Congruence
b. Unconditional positive regard
c. Empathy
d. Transference

64. Which of the following is NOT true about the use of advisory councils in an ASCA National Model program?

a. Advisory councils must meet quarterly each school year.
b. Advisory councils can assist the school counselor in reviewing program results.
c. Advisory councils should include students and parents.
d. Advisory councils should be smaller than 20 members.

65. Mrs. Jones is a high school counselor working with a student in individual counseling. The student is struggling with math class and recently received a failing grade on an exam. In the counseling session, the student makes the statement, "I failed my math test. I am so stupid!" If Mrs. Jones is taking a cognitive behavioral therapy-based approach with this student, which of the following would be an appropriate response to the student's statement?

a. Challenging the student's belief that they must be stupid if they received a failing grade on a test
b. Asking the student about their previous experiences with math tests to explore the root of the student's struggles
c. Asking the student if there has been a math test they performed well on and trying to identify what the student did differently on that test
d. Reflecting the student's statement, validating their feelings, and demonstrating unconditional positive regard for the student

66. A 2nd-grade student recently mastered the skill of adding two-digit numbers. His teacher knows that, because of his mastery of addition, he is ready to learn the process of subtracting two-digit numbers with her support and guidance. The teacher is basing her understanding of the student's learning on which concept?

a. Assimilation and accommodation
b. Zone of proximal development
c. Social learning
d. Classical conditioning

67. Brianna is a 3rd-grade student whose teacher reports that she regularly interrupts classroom instruction by getting up out of her seat and "wandering around the room." Which of the following methods for collecting data would provide the most useful information for creating an intervention for Brianna?

a. A tally sheet to record the number of times the behavior occurs in a day
b. A functional behavior assessment to determine the function of the behavior
c. A checklist to record the number of times the behavior occurs and in which situations
d. An observation by a staff member to take notes about the behavior

68. A counselor is leading an assertiveness training group based on cognitive behavioral therapy. Which of the following techniques would most likely be used in this specific type of group?

a. Role-playing
b. Linking and encouraging
c. Unstructured techniques
d. Empty chair

69. What is the purpose of demographic information on survey assessments?

a. It has no real purpose.
b. This information should not be included.
c. It helps to identify differences.
d. It helps to identify similarities.

70. A state requires all of its students to take an assessment each year that measures mastery of grade-level content standards taught during the year. This type of assessment is best described as which of the following?

a. Achievement test
b. Aptitude test
c. Placement test
d. Norm-referenced test

71. Parents can be involved in the school in a number of ways. You would like to increase parent participation in the career resource room at the school. In addition to contacting the PTA, how else might a counselor recruit parents to volunteer?

a. Distribute annual surveys for parents to identify their volunteer interests and abilities.
b. The PTA is the only place to find volunteers.
c. Place an ad in the newspaper.
d. Recruit teachers because they are easier to contact.

72. A counselor is a covered mental health provider under the Health Insurance Portability and Accountability Act of 1996 (HIPAA). As such, their clients have a right to:

a. Contest payment for services if records show that inadequate progress has been made
b. Request to have their protected electronic health records amended
c. Receive a copy of their diagnostic summary, treatment plan, and psychotherapy notes
d. Prevent the counselor from contacting family members in the event of a serious and imminent threat

73. A 16-year-old female with an intellectual disability reports chewing up her food, regurgitating it, and then rechewing it, reswallowing it, or spitting it out. Her symptoms are likely to meet the diagnostic criteria for:

a. Bulimia nervosa
b. Pica
c. Binge eating disorder
d. Rumination disorder

74. A test is considered standardized when certain components of the test and testing environment are the same among test-takers. In order for a test to be standardized, all of the following components are required to be the same EXCEPT:

a. The length of time given to take the test
b. The age of the individuals taking the test
c. The number of questions on the test
d. The instructions given when taking the test

75. Which of the following is NOT an appropriate academic advising activity for a school counselor?

a. Interpreting achievement tests
b. Keeping academic records
c. Interpreting student records
d. Analyzing grades in relation to achievement

76. According to the ASCA National Model, which of the following tasks related to assisting students with post-secondary plans is an appropriate activity for a school counselor?

a. Calculating class rank and grade point average
b. Coordinating schoolwide SAT testing
c. Assisting students with understanding course selections
d. Copying records needed for college applications

77. Of the following, which form of emotional regulation is associated with higher rates of psychopathology?

a. Response-focused modulation
b. Antecedent-focused modulation
c. Cognitive reappraisal
d. Situation modification

78. A school counselor conducts a needs assessment with students and staff. Using the data gathered from the needs assessment, the counselor could do all of the following EXCEPT:

a. Identify small-group counseling topics
b. Design classroom guidance curriculum
c. Identify individual student needs
d. Evaluate the previous year's program

79. Which of the following is NOT an appropriate use of end-of-grade standardized test scores?

a. Identifying an individual student's academic strengths
b. Improving classroom instructional plans
c. Determining eligibility for special education services
d. Tracking an individual student's academic growth

80. A counselor is asked to speak to a group of Junior Rangers about future career choices, and plan a presentation based upon knowledge of one of the members of the group. What type of reasoning is the counselor employing?

a. Operant rationalization
b. Deductive reasoning
c. Inductive reasoning
d. Constructive reasoning

Answer Key and Explanations for Test #1

1. A: Traditional counseling programs tend to focus on issues after something has occurred. In the given situation, this crisis intervention program is probably reserved for students who have recently experienced some type of personal crisis. In a developmental counseling model, the counselor will develop programs to meet the needs of students by using a full-service approach. This counselor may implement crisis prevention as well as intervention programs. By including a crisis prevention program, the counselor is meeting the needs of at-risk students. This program will assist these students in avoiding potential crisis situations by offering various emotional and cognitive skills that these students may not already possess.

2. A: The annual calendar identifies the major activities of the school counseling program and publishes them in a manner that is accessible to stakeholders. The annual calendar can be used by the school counselor to increase the visibility of their comprehensive school counseling program and help stakeholders understand the components of the program. Activities include classroom guidance lessons, parent nights, student or class meeting dates, standardized test dates, college information meetings or application deadlines, and family activities.

The annual agreement is an ASCA National Model document that is used to outline the school counseling program and establish a formal agreement between the school counselor and school administration regarding counseling program goals. It is typically not a document that stakeholders outside of the counselor and principal have access to. The school data profile is a template used by the school counselor to identify areas of strength and need in their student achievement and behavior data, which can then be used to create action plans or program goals. Finally, a curriculum action plan is a document used by the school counselor to design the classroom guidance program and align the program with curricular goals, but this is not a document that is typically communicated to various stakeholders.

3. A: Beginning a solution-focused brief counseling session involves having the student define the problem and determine their desired goals for the counseling. With the assistance of the counselor, the intervention or behavior change is both determined and initiated by the student. Strategic tasks are assigned by the counselor and involve a direct behavior change. For example, if a student is having difficulty with academics and has a goal to raise his grades, then a strategic task would be for him to study for one hour every night. In subsequent counseling sessions, the counselor would offer support and positive feedback in order to encourage the student to reach his academic goals. Once the goals for that particular problem have been reached, the sessions are no longer required, and counseling is terminated.

4. B: Classroom guidance is the only component that fits the criteria described in the question. All students benefit from the developmentally appropriate curriculum provided by the school counselor during classroom guidance lessons. In fact, this systematic method of reaching all students is one of the main benefits of providing a classroom guidance curriculum. For ASCA Mindsets and Behaviors, which all students are expected to demonstrate mastery of, classroom guidance provides a method to reach each student.

5. B: Almost all parents believe that they have well-behaved, intelligent children; therefore, some parents are quick to become defensive and unwilling to listen when schools call regarding problems with their children. As a counselor, it often falls on you to set up parent conferences. It is important to keep in mind the feelings and beliefs of the parents as well as the policies of the school. By speaking to parents with openness and allowing them to be a part of decision-making processes, the counselor allows a partnership to develop. By creating this sense of partnership and cooperation, the counselor keeps the student's best interests in focus.

6. A: Counselors can be responsible for more than just the mental and emotional well-being of students. When a school offers various career development programs, students who participate gain valuable skills for the future. On-the-job training programs are an excellent way to increase job skills. Additionally, these programs often help students decide what career path to follow. These programs allow students to go to school and work while earning school credits and gaining practical business experience. Counselors must understand that cooperation and communication with the community and leaders in the business community can be the key to success for these types of programs.

7. B: According to Ginzberg and associates, the three stages of career development are fantasy (birth to age 11), tentative (ages 11 to 17), and realistic (ages 17 to adulthood). In this case, based on age, Sophie would be in the fantasy stage of development. Growth would be an appropriate answer choice based on Sophie's age, but that is not a stage in career development theory. Instead, growth is one of five developmental stages identified by Super.

8. C: School counselors should never be the sole decision-makers in any part of the IEP process; instead, they should serve as members of a multi-disciplinary team working together to meet the needs of students with special needs. According to ASCA, school counselors provide only short-term, goal-focused counseling as an IEP-related service; long-term or therapeutic counseling should be provided by other qualified mental health professionals (e.g., school psychologists, social workers, or community providers) rather than being written into an IEP as a school counselor service. Writing and determining the specific social-emotional goals in the IEP is the responsibility of the entire IEP team and typically the special education case manager; the school counselor contributes data and suggestions but does not unilaterally write IEP goals. Therefore, (C) is not an accurate description of the counselor's role, whereas (A), (B), and (D) are.

9. C: The influence of peer relationships, personal beliefs, and environmental factors is known as reciprocal determinism. Reciprocal determinism is the foundational concept of Bandura's social learning theory, or social cognitive theory (SCT). SCT has been used along with attachment theory, interpersonal theory, and feminist theory to study factors related to adolescent dating and relationships. Lev Semyonovich Vygotsky used the term *zone of proximal development* to describe the difference between what a child does independently and what they can do with help. This concept is used to explore ways to teach reading, writing, and other language skills. Sigmund Freud used the term *pleasure principle* when explaining the role of the id in personality development. Psychological hedonism states that all human behavior is dictated by actions directed toward attaining pleasure or avoiding pain.

10. A: The ASVAB is an aptitude test designed to measure a student's strengths in relation to potential careers in the military. As the name suggests, aptitude tests are designed to measure an individual's aptitude or potential for success. Aptitude tests are frequently used in career planning or guidance, as many examples of aptitude tests (such as the ASVAB, Holland Code Career Aptitude Test, and Myers-Briggs Career Type Indicator) point test-takers to certain careers or fields based on their individual strengths. End-of-grade tests are an example of an achievement test, or one which measures what the test-taker has learned. The SAT, while originally designed as an aptitude test, was redesigned in 2016 and is now another example of an achievement test. The TOEFL is a proficiency test that measures the test-taker's English language ability as compared to a general standard.

11. B: Although FERPA permits sharing academic information within the school for staff with a "legitimate educational interest," outside agencies do not qualify for this permission. Although sharing this information with the case manager would probably directly benefit the student by assisting the tutoring program with identifying areas of need, the counselor must have parental consent to share this information with any outside agency. Having the student choose whether to provide this information is not appropriate, especially if they are a minor.

12. A: Preferential seating is a classroom accommodation that allows for a child to be seated in an area of the classroom that best addresses their needs; in this case, preferential seating may include the child sitting near the board for the best chance at seeing what is written. Extended time is a classroom accommodation, but the connection between difficulty seeing what is written on the board and providing extended time is not clear. Wearing glasses would probably help, but this does not describe a classroom accommodation, as glasses are not provided in the classroom. Cues or reminders to wear prescription glasses may be a good strategy for the student described, but only if forgetting to wear glasses is an issue. Finally, small group instruction describes an intervention or instructional strategy, not a classroom accommodation. In addition, the link between not being able to see the board and small group instruction is not very clear.

13. B: Advisory councils are a part of the Manage component of the ASCA National Model and are utilized to help develop programs that are reflective of the school's needs. While students are involved in the advisory council process, it is not a direct or indirect student service under the Deliver component.

14. C: Kohlberg's Theory of Moral Development involves the development of an individual's ethics, values, and principles. This theory consists of three levels: pre-conventional, conventional, and post conventional. In the pre-conventional level, children learn morals and values through obedience and punishment. For instance, children learn that it is not acceptable to hit others when they are punished for hitting a sibling. In the conventional level, youth learn through conformity and social order. Individuals learn by observing the world around them and understanding social norms. Finally, in the post-conventional level, individuals learn through universally accepted ethical considerations.

15. D: Students who identify as LGBTQ are more likely to have poor grades and patterns of truancy than their heterosexual peers. Students in this group also report feeling less safe at school and are more likely to be bullied, all factors that can aggravate academic outcomes. Studies have found that some of these impacts are significant. These are important trends for school counselors to be aware of. Effective school counselors can help LGBTQ youth to establish protective factors (such as connecting with peers or school staff) that can mitigate some of these potential negative impacts and help create a safe learning environment for all students through advocacy.

16. D: Pragmatics is mastered when a child can use language for different purposes, including greetings, requests, comments, or to provide answers to questions. Phonology refers to language and systems of sound. Semantics describes rules used for identifying the intended meaning of a word or phrase. Syntax is used when combining words to make sentences.

17. B: When determining group size, it is important to keep in mind the goals of the group as well as the age of the participants. Participants should have the opportunity to share and participate regularly, lest they lose interest or feel frustrated at waiting for their turn; they should also have ample opportunity to practice new skills to cement their new knowledge. Adult groups could successfully maintain a larger number of participants (up to 12, but 10 or fewer is ideal), but younger children require a smaller group. Four to six is a typical group size for elementary-age children.

18. D: Commonly used intelligence tests are frequently criticized for having cultural biases that impact an individual's outcome; in addition, intelligence tests are known to measure a very limited type of intelligence. Even with these limitations, intelligence tests can be a helpful tool when utilized as a part of a broader assessment of an individual. For example, when evaluating students for special education services, a child's score on the Wechsler Intelligence Scale for Children may indicate relative strengths and weaknesses in different measurements of intelligence, which can help pinpoint specific learning disabilities. It is important to keep in mind, however, the criticism of these tests for being culturally biased and understand that they may not measure intelligence in the same way across different cultures. Like most assessments, intelligence tests should not be used as the only data point for decision making.

19. B: Frank Parsons developed the trait-factor approach to career counseling. The trait-factor approach utilizes data from tests to match an individual with one best career. Therefore, a strictly trait-factor approach would begin with testing to determine Grace's traits. Trait-factor approaches do not rely on objective data from conversations. The Self-Directed Search from answer choice D refers to a tool used in John Holland's personality theory of career counseling.

20. A: According to the ACA Code of Ethics (2014), "Counselors limit the total or partial access of clients to their records only when there is compelling evidence that such access would cause harm to the client." If a client requires assistance with interpreting their records, counselors take the necessary time to provide that assistance. Counselors "prepare a plan for the transfer of clients and the dissemination of records to an identified colleague or records custodian in the case of the counselor's incapacitation, death, retirement, or termination of practice" (ACA, 2014). In situations involving multiple clients, counselors must "provide individual clients with only those parts of records that relate directly to them and do not include confidential information related to any other client" (ACA, 2014).

21. A: Teacher advisors cooperate with school counselors to provide students with all-around support. These advisors help students adjust to a new school by offering orientation and support. Additionally, teacher advisors provide students with a sounding board when resolving disputes or misunderstandings with faculty members or other students. Often, advisors will initiate student work groups for various issues students may experience. These groups may focus on communication, conflict resolution, or general adjustment strategies. Overall, teacher advisors serve as advocates for students in order to make school and the educational experience both pleasant and rewarding.

22. B: Positive uncertainty is H.B. Gelatt's later model of career decision-making. According to Bandura, personal agency reflects an individual's ability to achieve objectives. Self-efficacy is Bandura's term for an individual's belief that one can succeed at something. Vicarious learning is one of several learning experiences that Bandura states can strengthen self-efficacy.

23. D: This situation most likely calls for an intermediate intervention. Broad, proactive measures such as a parent information night or classroom guidance likely would not address the needs of this specific group of students who are already failing classes. In many schools, this would be considered a tier II intervention, which is a more targeted intervention for students who are exhibiting academic difficulties. A special education referral would not be appropriate at this level, as other intermediate interventions have not yet been put into place.

24. B: Each of the symptoms described could be indicative of a vision problem. Before moving to a full educational evaluation for learning disabilities or other learning problems, a simple vision screening could help the student described overcome a barrier to learning. In many districts, a vision screening is a required step in the intervention process prior to any special education or psychological referrals. The behaviors described do not necessarily point to abuse or neglect, although the school social worker can be a resource in procuring free or low-cost medical eye exams and eyeglasses for students who do not pass their vision screening.

25. A: The define component contains these standards. The define component of the ASCA National Model seeks to define school counseling as a profession and sets the parameters for quality school counseling programs. The manage component of the model aims to provide school counselors with the frameworks and tools they need to make their school counseling program successful. The deliver component of the model helps school counselors provide appropriate services to their students, directly or indirectly, in order to improve student achievement and behavior. The assess component of the model encourages school counselors to regularly assess their school counseling activities to ensure they are effective.

26. C: One major benefit of ASCA membership is access to their extensive research database, including research on counselor effectiveness, best practices, and student outcomes. Each of the other resources mentioned may have this type of research, but ASCA will have the most extensive collection for counselors.

27. D: In Kohlberg's Punishment-Obedience stage, an individual will not distinguish between doing right and simply avoiding punishment. This stage applies directly in this situation, as the student would comply with rules solely as a means to avoid the negative consequence of receiving detention. Answer A, Personal Reward, refers primarily to instances in which an individual is motivated to attain or achieve something. Answer B, Law and Order, refers to an appeal to maintain the social order and supersedes individual interests. Answer C, Good Boy-Nice Girl, refers to a stage in which intention is taken into account above action alone. In this stage, being liked or having a good reason is a motivating factor, even in an otherwise morally wrong situation. The student in this situation is only described as avoiding a negative consequence rather than having any pleasing rewards or societal devotion for following the rules, leaving answer D as the only possible correct answer.

28. C: Cognitive behavioral therapy is rooted in the belief that a client's emotional state is directly related to their beliefs or thoughts about their problems. Much of a client's time within cognitive behavioral therapy is spent challenging cognitions and changing self-talk, which in turn results in changing the client's emotional state. Don't confuse the ABC model in cognitive behavioral therapy with the ABC behavior model often used in schools when developing behavior interventions.

29. B: Making a broad announcement about the student's arrival is likely to embarrass the student and possibly create more alienation from the general student body. As this student does not necessarily have a problem, direct counseling and education may not beneficial. School counselors who offer supportive services to the student and her family will be the most beneficial in easing the transition from one school to the next. Counselors can enlist support and assistance from other students by providing the new student a peer guide for the first couple of days. The guide will show her around the school and make sure the student knows where her classes are. This guide can also provide information about the school, such as the various clubs and sports available and upcoming events. Additional support from the school and the community will provide the student and her family with important information about the school and the new area.

30. B: The brother is in Piaget's preoperational stage of cognitive development. Children in the preoperational stage are between the ages of 2 and 7. Children in this stage have difficulty operationalizing or manipulating information, which makes the task of conservation difficult. Conservation is the notion that changing the shape or size of something does not change the object if nothing additional is added or taken away. The brother assumed that his sister received two cookies, and he received only one. A child in the sensorimotor stage of cognitive development is between the ages of birth and age 2. Children in the sensorimotor stage engage in symbolic thinking. The concrete operational stage describes children aged 7-11 who can perform mental operations. Finally, children older than age 11 are capable of formal operations, including logic and reasoning.

31. B: Dual relationships occur when a counselor and client know each other prior to beginning a counseling relationship. In the school setting, this may occur if the counselor has family members in the same school. In these cases, the counselor should refer their family members to another counselor if possible. In the situation described above, inviting a student to talk outside of school creates a dual relationship and violates professional guidelines against using a school to promote or benefit any private practice or non-school counseling activities. This situation also illustrates that the counselor is crossing professional boundaries by suggesting that they meet over coffee.

32. C: While potential group members often do want to know who else will be in their group, disclosing the names of other group members is not part of the informed consent process. In acquiring informed consent from group members, an understanding of the purpose and goals of the group, the risks and limitations of the group, limits of confidentiality in a group setting, and training and qualifications of the counselor are all topics that should be explained to and understood by the group members. In a school setting with minors, parental consent is also necessary for informed consent.

33. A: Conducting a program evaluation is an important component of a comprehensive school counseling program, and sharing the results is part of the evaluation process. According to ASCA, the goals of sharing these results are to "promote understanding, increase the value of and promote respect and indispensability for the work of professional school counselors." ASCA recommends sharing with a variety of stakeholders, including faculty, administrators, and community members. Therefore, those methods that effectively communicate counseling program results to a wide variety of stakeholders in a clear, easy-to-access, and easy-to-understand format are the most desirable methods.

34. D: Communication is not a category for the function of a behavior. While many would say that all behavior is a form of communication, the function of the behavior is what the individual is trying to accomplish with the behavior. Behavior may be an attempt to escape or avoid something unpleasant such as tasks, people, or environments; to gain or access something desirable like attention, control, or tangibles (such as toys); or for sensory input such as stimulation or regulation. Different functional behavior assessment forms may use slightly different terms (such as "avoidance" instead of "escape"), but the functions almost always fall in these categories.

35. A: Bronfenbrenner's ecological systems theory proposed that, as children grow, the various environments (systems) in which they function interact to influence their development. Therefore, in order to understand a child's development, all of the systems must be evaluated. Bronfenbrenner proposed the following five ecological systems, ranging from the most intimate to the broadest: microsystem, mesosystem, exosystem, macrosystem, chronosystem.

36. B: In this situation, the counselor's goal should be to stop the inappropriate conversation. Gossiping about others who are not in the group is not helpful to the group or appropriate in the context of the group. Blocking is a strategy for stopping a hurtful behavior. Clarification, linking, and active listening would all be inappropriate choices in this scenario because they would invite the student to continue their line of discussion.

37. A: Scaling questions are a key component of solution-focused brief counseling and are used to help the client notice improvements toward their goal. Other examples of solution-focused brief counseling techniques include asking about exceptions, the miracle question, and assigning homework suggestions. Free association is a technique more typically utilized by a classical psychoanalyst (such as Sigmund Freud). Changing self-talk is commonly associated with rational-emotive behavior therapy (Albert Ellis), which assumes that the root of the client's emotional disturbance lies in their irrational thoughts, and therefore changing cognitions can change the client's emotional state. The empty chair technique is a Gestalt technique (Fritz Perls) where the client directs conversation about their thoughts and feelings toward an empty chair as if the person they are speaking to is sitting in it.

38. A: The ASCA National Model states the question to be answered by the program evaluation as "How are students different as a result of the school counseling program?" Within the program evaluation, data about academic achievement, progress toward stated goals and objectives, counselor use of time, and the effectiveness of program components is collected and evaluated, but the impact on students is the focus of the evaluation process. Measuring student impact allows the school counselor to understand their progress toward stated goals and to identify areas for improvement or adjustments to their counseling program.

39. D: Human relations training offers students the opportunity to see each other as individuals. This type of training serves to increase students' understanding of one another. In the given situation, there appears to be a lot of racial tension, which is leading to regular fighting. When a school offers students human relations training, they will learn to view each other as human beings rather than racial stereotypes. This training should serve to increase cultural understanding and decrease the current level of fighting in the classroom. This situation may prompt a counselor to study the school overall to see if this behavior is occurring elsewhere. If so, a school-wide human relations training program may be appropriate.

40. D: Piaget's stages of cognitive development are 1) sensorimotor (birth to 2 years) during which the child learns about himself and his environment through sensory perceptions and motor activities; 2) preoperational (2-7 years) in which language develops and the child is egocentric; 3) concrete operational (7-11 years) during which the child begins to think logically but still has trouble with abstract concepts; and 4) formal operational (11 years to adulthood) during which the child develops the capability of logical thought, deductive reasoning, and systematic planning.

41. D: Cognitive literacy skills teach students how to problem-solve and make decisions. Programs designed to address cognitive skills focus on critical thinking, analysis, evaluation, classification, and conceptualization. According to Bloom's taxonomy of learning, these skills are essential in the education process. Schools can use organizational planners for homework and school events in order to teach some of these skills. As students develop their cognitive skills, their study skills will also improve. Finally, cognitive skills development can also focus on self-regulation and self-monitoring. These abilities allow the student to think about their actions and the consequences of those actions.

42. A: The Wechsler Intelligence Scale for Children (WISC) is a commonly used tool in a psycho-educational evaluation, typically as part of a special education evaluation; however, it is inappropriate to use an intelligence test as the sole basis for special education placement decisions. For example, if a student has a suspected learning disability, an average or above-average IQ score should not be used to deny them special education services. It is also inappropriate to use IQ test results to choose students' coursework, career guidance, or college options. Assessments represent only one data point in making decisions about a student's education.

43. C: Cultural diversity education is important in all schools, regardless of demographics. In this situation, it could be argued that the counselor is acting in an unprofessional and possibly unethical manner. What this counselor is failing to understand is that culture extends beyond the color of someone's skin. Culture includes various lifestyles, family types, religious beliefs, and ethnicities. Even in a predominantly white school, many cultures may be observable. If the counselor in this situation were aware of her own culture as well as that of others, she might realize the importance of offering these programs to all students.

44. A: The mean is the average, so the average test score on this test is 50. The most common score is called the mode. Knowing the highest possible test score is useful in determining the range, which is the highest score minus the lowest score. The percentage of students who passed the test is useful information for instructional or curricular decisions and is called a passing rate or proficiency rate (usually with standardized end-of-grade tests).

45. D: Sublimation: The client redirects socially unacceptable impulses to acceptable actions, such as when the victim of a crime redirects anger toward becoming an advocate for other victims. **Regression**: The client retreats to an earlier stage of development, such as by being more dependent. **Suppression**: The client voluntarily blocks unpleasant emotions, such as by refusing to think about an event. **Repression**: The client involuntarily blocks unpleasant emotions, such as being unable to remember being raped.

46. B: Solution-focused brief counseling always focuses on the exception to the problem, improvements since the previous session, and progress toward the goal. Therefore, most subsequent sessions will begin with the counselor asking the client about what has improved since the previous session.

47. A: Even though termination is the final stage of the group counseling process, an effective group leader will begin to prepare group members for the termination in the selection and screening process by explaining the duration and goals of the group.

48. D: Teachers, along with other helping professionals such as counselors, nurses, and physical therapists, closely align with the social personality type. Examples of the other personality types include: realistic (pilot, surveyor), investigative (astronomer, physician), artistic (writer, designer), enterprising (lawyer, salesperson), and conventional (accountant, actuary).

49. D: ASCA has a variety of position statements that touch on academic topics, including course selection. A school counselor should use a variety of data sources when assisting with student academic planning, so using grades and standardized test data alone is not an appropriate strategy. Many school counselors may find themselves in the position where their school or district policy requires course selections to be based on grades and test scores, and in those situations, the counselor would act as an advocate for systemic change. A comprehensive school counseling program will likely use multiple strategies for facilitating course selections at any level. Grade-level meetings and/or classroom guidance lessons are very common ways to facilitate the course selection process, but counselors should keep in mind their students' background knowledge and comfort with the course selection process when opting for these strategies. In addition, students may have individual needs or specific questions that would be missed in these whole-group formats. Depending on the counselor's caseload, having individual meetings with each student and their parents may not be feasible, but there are usually individual students for whom this is appropriate.

50. B: A needs assessment is a type of perception data that is commonly used to plan a comprehensive school counseling program. Needs assessments help a counselor identify areas of strength and need in their school in order to make decisions about programming. Although the school data profile is another helpful document outlining data that can be used to plan a school counseling program, it is not a type of perception data. The school data profile focuses on demographic and outcome data. Pre-test data is a type of perception data, but it wouldn't be used to plan a comprehensive school counseling program; instead, pre-test data could be used to evaluate prior knowledge of a topic or to compare to the post-test data to establish the effectiveness of an intervention. Finally, achievement testing data is a type of outcome data, and while it can be part of the planning process (for example, it is part of the school data profile), achievement testing data alone would not provide enough information to plan a comprehensive school counseling program.

51. C: Cultural bias is a potentially significant problem affecting the validity of tests and should be considered not only when selecting and administering tests but also when interpreting test results. Cultural bias occurs when differences in test-takers' gender, race, ethnicity, or socioeconomic status impact their background knowledge, understanding of test items, or understanding of the behaviors required to successfully complete a test. For example, a test that includes an English idiom in a math question may not be accessible for English language learners, and their success on that test item could be affected due to their English proficiency, rather than their math ability. A test item asking students to complete a phrase from a nursery rhyme may not be accessible to students from a culture that does not practice or sing that nursery rhyme, or a reading passage that references polo may be confusing for students who do not have background knowledge related to polo due to their socioeconomic status or culture. Differences in classroom groupings would not result in a cultural bias, but they could result in a difference in instructional quality or curriculum taught, which could affect student outcomes on tests.

52. A: Elementary school is the time when children are learning the most and developing important motor skills and mental functions. Counselors must be able to recognize developmental delays, as well as advanced learners. School counselors will be major advocates for students who may experience developmental delays. While the other options may be important, these issues are more likely seen at the junior high and high school levels. Knowledge in continued education will be important for high school students who wish to pursue a college education; counselors with students in these age groups will need to educate students and offer assistance in applying to colleges and obtaining financial aid and scholarships. Additionally, relationship building, adjustment, and coping mechanisms are issues most often seen in junior high school, as these years are a time of many changes physically, emotionally, and educationally.

53. D: A diagnostic assessment for learning needs focuses on four main factors: prior knowledge, misconceptions, interests, and learning style preferences. The purpose of this type of assessment is to determine the student's strengths and weaknesses in order to develop an effective intervention strategy. Diagnostic assessments can be done in either formal or informal settings and in either individual or group settings. In the case of a formal setting, counselors can conduct a student survey or skills test. For informal settings, the counselor can simply ask a student or groups of students various questions pertaining to each factor. For example, a counselor may ask, "Do you like to learn by reading a book or seeing material presented in picture form?"

54. D: Kelly's symptoms could be consistent with ADHD. For a child to be diagnosed with ADHD, they must present with six or more symptoms, in at least two settings, for six months or more. Children can be diagnosed with a combined presentation (both inattentive and hyperactive-impulsive symptoms), predominantly inattentive presentation (six or more inattentive symptoms, but fewer than six hyperactive-impulsive symptoms), or predominantly hyperactive-impulsive presentation (six or more hyperactive-impulsive symptoms, but fewer than six inattentive symptoms). Since the description of Kelly's symptoms does not include any hyperactive-impulsive symptoms, it is likely that the symptoms being described align with a predominantly inattentive presentation. Task avoidance could be a symptom of generalized anxiety disorder or a specific learning disability, and forgetfulness could be an anxiety symptom. While some of the symptoms described align with the diagnoses listed in other answer choices, the six symptoms together describe a child who likely has ADHD.

55. A: The James-Lange Theory of Emotion was proposed in 1884. It is a combination of the ideas of William James and Carl Lange. The theory states that one's body reacts to a stimulus first and is then followed by the emotional reaction. For example, a spider lands on an individual's arm. The individual jumps and screams in reaction. The individual then interprets the body's reaction as fear, thus leading to actually feeling the emotion of fearfulness. This idea of the physiological response preceding the emotional one was new at the time, and one of the first theories used to explain the science of emotion.

56. C: According to Gottfredson, younger children tend to choose occupations that fit their sex. Gottfredson's theory is developmental. She stated that since children of this age tend to identify certain occupations with either the male or the female gender, it follows that they will choose occupations based on gender roles or stereotypes. Orientation to sex roles is the name of her second developmental stage (ages 6-8). Preadolescents tend to choose occupations consistent with their social values since they are in Gottfredson's stage of orientation to social valuation (ages 9-13). Children of this age may also rule out occupations they feel are inappropriate to their intelligence or levels of ability. Adolescents, who are in Gottfredson's stage of orientation to internal unique self (age 14 and older), tend to choose occupations based on their awareness of their own personal characteristics.

57. C: School counselors should always follow school and district policy when students are in crisis or expressing suicidal ideation; in instances where those policies are not safe or appropriate, counselors should advocate for policies to be changed. Students who express suicidal ideation should always be taken seriously, and counselors have a duty to warn a student's parents in order to protect the student. In the situation described, Amy appears to be actively in crisis, so an immediate referral to a professional for evaluation and support is appropriate. It does not appear that Amy has time to wait for her parents to make an appointment with a therapist. Without any expression of concerns about abuse or neglect at home, Child Protective Services would not be an appropriate referral. No-harm contracts and suicide contracts are not recommended, and they place the student at risk of harm and the counselor at risk of liability.

58. D: Counselors must respect the cultural identity of their students. Since the student is not seeing the counselor because of cultural identity issues, it would be considered professionally inappropriate for the counselor to focus on her Chinese heritage unprompted. It is, however, the counselor's responsibility to understand this student's cultural identity in order to develop effective interventions for this student's presenting problem. The counselor must also have a clear understanding of her own beliefs and stereotypes in this situation that may cause bias when treating this student. Counselors who are unaware of these issues may inadvertently treat a student of another culture with negativity or less support than she would a student of her own culture.

59. B: Bullies are at risk for a number of negative outcomes, including the increased potential to drop out of school. Counselors can implement many intervention strategies for bullying. School-wide interventions can include posted rules, announcements, and programs. Classroom interventions can involve the same intervention strategies as those implemented school wide, except on a smaller level. Individual interventions will address the student bully specifically. This type of intervention should be tailored to the individual and aim to define the root problem while providing education and intervention to change the negative behaviors. Referrals can also be made to anger management, communication, and conflict resolution programs.

60. B: Perspective taking is similar to empathy; however, it involves different mental processes. While a person can be empathic toward another, this function involves only an attempt to understand another person's feelings based on previous experience. Perspective taking involves more complex cognition. The individual involved in perspective taking will attempt to understand another's situation, analyze this situation, and gain an understanding of and respect for different points of view. Perspective taking is a useful activity for children requiring conflict resolution. By asking children to look at a situation from another person's point of view, they can begin to understand why there was conflict and possibly begin to formulate their own ideas for a resolution.

61. C: The student information system (SIS) is a very important resource for data-driven school counselors. Many data points essential to program evaluation activities can be found within this system, including individual, subgroup, and schoolwide data. Outcome data, in particular, is usually found within the SIS, including attendance rates, promotion and retention rates, graduation rates, student grade point averages, discipline referrals, suspensions, test scores, and so on. Process data, such as the information described in answer choice C, and perception data are typically harder to pull from the SIS and are more likely to be found in surveys, pre- and post-tests, sign-in sheets, needs assessments, and so forth. Each of these types of data is essential to a comprehensive program evaluation.

62. B: The individual's relative competence is NOT one of the factors identified by career self-efficacy theory as likely to be affected by the individual's expectations. This theory states that the individual's expectations will influence: 1) choice or whether a behavior will be initiated; 2) performance, or how much effort will be expended; and, 3) persistence, or to what extent the individual will persevere when confronted by obstacles. Some theorists believe these explain gender differences in career choices. Higher self-efficacy seems related to choice and persistence in math and science careers.

63. D: Carl Rogers' person-centered therapy, also known as client-centered therapy or nondirective counseling, focuses on three key factors: congruence, also known as genuineness or authenticity; unconditional positive regard, the concept of the therapist accepting the client no matter what they do; and empathy, or the therapist's ability to feel what the client is feeling. According to Rogers, if these three required conditions are met in an effective helping relationship, the client can develop positively. Transference describes the scenario in which a client projects their feelings or emotions onto the therapist.

64. A: Advisory councils are recommended to meet at least twice per year, but they are certainly not required to meet quarterly. No matter the frequency, the advisory council should utilize an agenda and meeting minutes to keep the meetings on track. Advisory councils can assist school counselors with a variety of tasks, including advising on program goals, reviewing program results, making recommendations for future program goals, and advocating for the school counseling program. School counselors are encouraged to recruit a diverse group of stakeholders to participate in an advisory council, and the recommended size is 8–20 members.

65. A: Cognitive behavioral therapy focuses on changing irrational thoughts that lead to unwanted or negative feelings. In this scenario, the counselor would challenge the student's belief that they received a failing grade on their math test because there is something inherently wrong with them or their intelligence. Instead, the counselor may help the student reframe their difficulty, such as by saying, "I received a failing grade on my math test because I did not prepare and study effectively." Meanwhile, answer choice B would be a problem-focused approach, and choice C reflects a more solution-focused approach. Choice D represents a person-centered approach.

66. B: The zone of proximal development describes the concepts or skills beyond what a learner is able to do on their own, or the "zone" where the learner can accomplish a new task or skill with the help of someone else. This is a key component of Vygotsky's social development theory.

67. C: A simple checklist to record the number of times the target behavior occurs, as well as a way to record the circumstances surrounding the behavior (such as time of day, type of instruction, or level of structure), would be useful to help the intervention team. This would help to notice trends or patterns and identify environmental or procedural modifications that could support appropriate behavior. A simple tally sheet, however, would not provide enough detail about the behavior to develop an intervention. A tally sheet may be appropriate to document improvements in the target behavior once an intervention is in place. In this situation, a functional behavior assessment is premature. Functional behavior assessments are appropriate for high-intensity behaviors or those behaviors that have not responded to lower-level interventions. While observations can be useful in many situations, they are typically utilized to supplement other types of data rather than used as stand-alone data.

68. A: Assertiveness training groups are typically highly structured and focus on practicing skills learned in the group through role-playing. Linking and encouraging may be used in many types of groups, so it is not specific to an assertiveness training cognitive behavioral therapy (CBT) group. The empty chair technique could be used in assertiveness training, but it is a Gestalt technique, not a CBT technique.

69. C: Typically, a counselor will conduct a student survey in order to gain an overall view of the student body. By collecting demographic information, the counselor can determine important differences in the student body. This information will assist in developing additional programs, activities, or interventions. When conducted as a formative assessment, demographic information can provide an indication of whether different groups of students are finding more benefit in a particular program or intervention. Again, this information will allow the counselor to modify a program or add programs to better fit the needs of all students involved.

70. A: Achievement tests measure how well the test-taker has mastered specific skills or objectives. End-of-grade or end-of-course tests, as required by many states and school districts, are examples of achievement tests because they measure a student's mastery of the content objectives or skills that are generally expected to be taught during that grade level or course. While some schools may use data from these achievement tests to make placement decisions for future courses, that is not what these types of tests are designed for. Aptitude tests are a different type of assessment that attempts to predict the test-taker's aptitude or future success in a specific area, while placement tests measure the test-taker's skill level in a specific content area in order to determine their current level for course placements. Norm-referenced tests measure the individual test-taker's or group of test-takers' results against another group of test-takers, while criterion-referenced tests measure the individual test-taker's results against a specific set of standards. For example, a norm-referenced test may indicate that a student's mathematics ability is more or less advanced than a group of their same-aged peers, while a criterion-referenced test would simply indicate that a student has mastered all of their current grade-level mathematics standards.

71. A: Annual surveys are an easy and effective way to learn about the level of participation, interests, and abilities of parents. These surveys can be sent to parents at the beginning of the year and offer parents the opportunity to volunteer for long- or short-term projects. Surveys should include information about the parents' willingness to participate, their availability, and any special skills they may have. A preliminary list of volunteer events or projects should also be included in these surveys so that parents can select opportunities that correspond with their schedules and interests. By reaching beyond the PTA for support and assistance, schools will develop lasting partnerships with parents and improve the learning environment for the students.

72. B: HIPAA grants clients the right to request that a "covered entity" amend their electronic healthcare record. Professional counselors who use electronic health records to transmit health information in a transactional capacity (e.g., to bill insurance) qualify as a covered entity under HIPAA. Counselors have the right to deny the amendment if they determine that the client's healthcare record is accurate and complete. Payment for services must be agreed upon at the onset of treatment and cannot be contested based on the client's inadequate progress. Under HIPAA, clients may receive a copy of their records, including diagnostic summaries and treatment plans. However, psychotherapy notes are considered to be an exemption. Psychotherapy notes are a counselor's personal notes and are typically not a part of the client's medical record. When the client poses a serious and imminent threat to themselves or others, counselors can contact family members without client authorization.

73. D: Rumination disorder is characterized by repeated regurgitation of food for at least 1 month. Individuals with rumination disorder engage in rechewing, reswallowing, and spitting their food out. Infants and older individuals with intellectual disabilities are more likely to be diagnosed with rumination disorder. Individuals with bulimia nervosa discreetly consume amounts of food that are larger than most individuals would eat in the same time period. This is followed by inappropriate compensatory behaviors (e.g., excessive exercise, self-induced vomiting, refusing to eat, or misusing diuretics). Individuals with pica ingest nonnutritive substances (e.g., paint, plaster, or clay). Finally, binge eating disorder includes recurrent episodes of binge eating, eating until uncomfortably full, or socially isolating when eating.

74. B: For a test to be standardized, the test questions, instructions, and testing procedures need to be consistent. Educators who administer standardized tests such as the SAT or end-of-grade tests are likely familiar with the requirements to read instructions from a script, carefully time the test administration, and maintain the consistency of the test format among test-takers. The age of the test-takers, however, has no impact on the standardization of the test itself. For example, many younger students take the SAT as part of gifted education programs or for practice for the future. If standardized test results are norm-referenced, the ages of test-takers could affect the norming group, but they do not affect the standardization of the test itself.

75. B: According to ASCA, clerical tasks, including maintaining student records, are inappropriate activities for school counselors. Appropriate tasks include interpretation of records and data.

76. C: Assisting students with course selections to help students make choices that are rigorous and align with their post-secondary plans is an appropriate activity for a school counselor. Understanding appropriate and inappropriate counseling tasks is a major focus of the Management section of the ASCA National Model; this is an area that school counselors should be very familiar with in order to plan their use of time and advocate for appropriate duties. A comprehensive school counseling program designed with the ASCA National Model will focus on prevention, intervention, and advocacy, not clerical or administrative tasks. When it comes to assisting students with post-secondary plans, there are many tasks that school counselors may have done historically or may still do in some schools that are not considered appropriate activities. These include tasks such as calculating class rank or grade point average, coordinating schoolwide SAT testing, copying student records for college applications, or doing other clerical tasks related to college applications.

77. A: Response-focused modulation is associated with higher rates of psychopathology. Response-focused emotional modulation, also known as suppression, occurs after one experiences an emotion. Response-focused emotional regulation inhibits the expression of an emotion, which does not change the emotion but instead changes the outcome. Antecedent-focused modulation, also known as cognitive appraisal, is associated with fewer instances of psychopathology. There are four strategies for antecedent-focused modulation: "situation selection, situation modification, attention deployment, cognitive change" (Gross, 2014). Cognitive reappraisal is a form of antecedent-focused modulation.

78. D: A well-designed needs assessment can be a powerful tool for school counselors in identifying areas of need, defining goals, and planning programming. Needs assessments can also identify areas where there may be equity gaps, individual student concerns, or common student concerns that may be addressed by small-group counseling. While it may be tempting to use a needs assessment to track changes in data from year to year as a form of program evaluation, this is not the purpose for which they are designed, and they are unlikely to be effective for program evaluation due to changes in student enrollment or staffing from year to year and a lack of specificity within the questions to evaluate individual programs.

79. C: Special education evaluations should be comprehensive evaluations that utilize a variety of data from multiple sources. End-of-grade standardized test scores should never be the sole data point to qualify or disqualify a child from receiving special education services.

80. C: Reasoning is a means by which one processes information in order to reach a conclusion. There are several forms of reasoning, two of which are inductive reasoning and deductive reasoning. Inductive reasoning is reasoning that flows from the specific to the general, such as knowing something about one member of a group, and then generalizing that to the entire group the individual belongs to. Deductive reasoning is the opposite. In deductive reasoning, knowledge of a particular group is generalized to each of the individuals within that group. It is of course, not best to rely on only one type of reasoning to reach a conclusion.

Practice Test #2

1. Which of the following is NOT considered a major developmental task of children and adolescents?

a. Sense of identity
b. Autonomy
c. Self-esteem
d. Knowledge acquisition

2. An elementary school counselor is conducting a small group focused on managing anger. In a session of the group, the counselor has students create a list of several strategies for dealing with anger and practice role-playing each one. During which stage of the small group process would this activity be most appropriate?

a. Initial/forming stage
b. Transition/storming stage
c. Working/norming stage
d. Termination/adjourning stage

3. A school counselor is creating a spreadsheet of student achievement data that includes end-of-grade test scores, graduation rates, and enrollment in honors courses. The counselor disaggregates the data by student subgroup. The counselor is most likely compiling this data for which of the following tasks?

a. Creating a closing-the-gap action plan
b. Creating a small-group action plan
c. Preparing the annual agreement
d. Conducting a needs assessment

4. In group interventions, there are typically three stages involved in the group dynamics: group formation, group awareness, and group action. What is the focus of the group formation stage?

a. To facilitate cooperation
b. To introduce all participants
c. To find out why everyone is in the group
d. To ask what group members hope to gain from the group

5. Joshua is a 5th-grade student who is frequently disruptive and explosive in the classroom. School-wide and classroom-wide interventions, such as positive recognition, class-based rewards, and modifying classroom procedures to reduce opportunities for inappropriate behavior have not resulted in an improvement in Joshua's behavior. Joshua's school counselor is working with the administrative team to develop a behavior plan for him. What would be the best method for collecting data to support the development of this plan?

a. Asking Joshua's teacher to write a narrative about his behavior throughout the school year and the interventions put into place
b. Collecting all of the discipline incident reports generated when Joshua was suspended throughout the year and looking for patterns
c. Asking Joshua's parents to complete a behavior checklist, indicating the behaviors they are most concerned about
d. Conducting a functional behavior assessment to determine the purpose of Joshua's behavior and factors contributing to it

6. Pre-post tests are important tools for assessments. What is the main thing to consider when developing a pre-post test?

a. Who will take the test
b. Key ideas and concepts
c. Number of questions
d. When to give the test

7. When beginning a program evaluation, what documentation will be necessary?

a. Satisfaction surveys from previous program sessions
b. A list of programs offered
c. The number of participants in last year's programs
d. Guidance curriculum guides

8. Classroom guidance is most often considered to be which type of counseling activity?

a. Prevention
b. Intervention
c. Outreach
d. Academic

9. In a private conversation with the school counselor, Mr. Morris, a high school teacher, said that he is concerned about bullying by students in his classroom. He reports that several students have been making comments about a student, Sally, during independent work, and refusing to allow her to join them during group work. Sally has been visibly upset after these interactions but has not made any complaints to Mr. Morris or other teachers. What should the school counselor do next?

a. Talk to the principal about the need to support Mr. Morris's classroom management.
b. Wait for Sally to make a report or complaint of bullying.
c. Ask Sally to come talk to the counselor in their office.
d. File a formal bullying complaint with the principal.

10. A school counselor is meeting with the parent of a student in order to discuss the parent's concerns about their child's academic progress. The parent is unsure of how to interpret their child's standardized test results from the state's end-of-grade, norm-referenced tests. Which of the following explanations of the child's test results is accurate for this type of test?

a. "Your child's percentile score compares their performance to their same-age peers across the state."
b. "Your child's percentile score indicates the number of test questions they answered correctly."
c. "Your child's percentile score indicates the percentage of grade-level standards they mastered this year."
d. "Your child's percentile score indicates their potential for success in the next grade level."

11. Which of the following would be considered an educational group?

a. A group focused on processing grief and loss.
b. A group focused on teaching parenting skills.
c. A group focused on planning a school event.
d. A group focused on overcoming test anxiety.

12. Which of the following is NOT an ASCA Mindsets & Behaviors for Student Success domain?

a. Career
b. Academic
c. Social/emotional
d. College readiness

13. Which of the following group counseling techniques can be used by a counselor to point out commonalities between group members, and thus improve group cohesion and interaction?

a. Clarification
b. Blocking
c. Linking
d. Active listening

14. Which of the following documents provides an outline of objectives that can be used in planning a classroom guidance curriculum?

a. ASCA Ethical Standards for School Counselors
b. ASCA Mindsets & Behaviors for Student Success
c. ASCA National Model
d. Recognized ASCA Model Program

15. Leslie is a middle school counselor who has an upcoming planning meeting with the counselor at the elementary school where the majority of Leslie's students attended. The purpose of the meeting is to begin planning for a successful middle school transition for Leslie's future students. Which of the following topics would likely NOT be discussed in this meeting?

a. Strategies for helping students take responsibility for their learning (study skills and organization)
b. Strategies for helping students integrate into their new school (clubs and activities)
c. An overview of the course selection, the registration process, and the data needed to complete selections
d. The IEP goals and services for EC students who will be entering Leslie's school next year

16. A fourth-grade student has a Section 504 plan providing accommodations to help the child transition from one activity to the next, keep an organized work area, and stay on task. A likely diagnosis would be:

a. Autism spectrum disorder (ASD)
b. Oppositional defiant disorder (ODD)
c. ADHD
d. Conduct disorder

17. Mr. Smith, a school counselor, is serving on an IEP team for a student with severe social-emotional needs. The IEP team brings up the need for the student to have individual counseling focused on these needs. Which of the following statements would be an appropriate response from Mr. Smith in this situation?

a. It is inappropriate for a school counselor to provide individual counseling to a student as part of their IEP, as they are not certified special education staff.
b. It is appropriate for a school counselor to provide individual counseling to a student as part of their IEP, but no more than once per week.
c. It is inappropriate for a school counselor to provide individual counseling to a student as part of their IEP, as it is not an approved special education service.
d. It is appropriate for a school counselor to provide individual counseling to a student as part of their IEP, but only on a short-term basis for a specific goal.

18. A school counselor completes a school data profile in order to plan their school counseling program. In analyzing the data gathered, the counselor notes that the school's graduation rate has gradually decreased over the last few years among students with disabilities. Based on the available data, what ASCA National Model document should the counselor use to address this concern?

a. Curriculum action plan
b. Small group action plan
c. Closing-the-gap action plan
d. Lesson plan

19. A career counseling client uses the Self-Directed Search (SDS) assessment instrument and receives a three-point Holland code of ESC. Which of the following occupations would give the client the highest job satisfaction?

a. Biologist
b. Business owner
c. Lawyer
d. Interior decorator

20. A school counselor is developing a list of community agencies for referrals for the upcoming school year. Which of the following is NOT a step the counselor should take in developing this list?

a. Contact each agency to determine if they are open and accepting new referrals.
b. Submit the list to the school or district for vetting and approval according to policy.
c. Make a list of the agencies current students and families utilize for counseling.
d. Gather information about the services each agency provides, including whether they accept insurance.

21. Counselors leading groups are ethically obligated to inform participants of the limits of confidentiality in a group setting. At which stage of the group counseling process should this disclosure take place?

a. Selection/screening
b. Initial/forming
c. Transition/storming
d. Working/norming

22. James is a middle school student in a counseling group. During a group session, the school counselor notices that James has been more withdrawn and has not been participating in the group discussion. Which of the following strategies would be an appropriate response to this observation?

a. Ignore James's non-participation, as group participation is voluntary.
b. Pull James aside during the group session and have a conversation with him about his participation.
c. Make a connection between James and another group member.
d. Remove James from the group, as his non-participation is threatening other group members' progress.

23. A counselor is researching best practices for working with a family whose children witnessed a violent crime and are now experiencing anxiety, having difficulty focusing, showing physical illness, and displaying inappropriate behavior. Which of the following research-based approaches would this counselor most likely consider in working with these children?

a. Family system therapy
b. Trauma-informed practices
c. Multi-tiered systems of support
d. Positive behavior intervention and support

24. Edgar Schein used which of the following terms to explain an individual's perception of their own values, skills, abilities, and interests in regard to work?

a. Active adjustments
b. Career anchors
c. Career congruence
d. Life role salience

25. A 14-year-old client is involved in a neighborhood gang, is truant, and is using drugs on a daily basis. Which treatment program would be most efficacious for this client?

a. The Incredible Years
b. Parent-implemented intervention
c. Self-help (e.g., 12-step groups)
d. Multisystemic therapy (MST)

26. Mr. Golden is a school counselor whose religious beliefs discourage same-sex relationships. A student shares in individual counseling that he is in a same-sex relationship. What is Mr. Golden's ethical obligation in working with this student?

a. Mr. Golden should refer the student to a different counselor within the school due to the bias his religious beliefs create.
b. Mr. Golden should share his bias with the student so that the student has a full understanding before giving informed consent.
c. Mr. Golden should seek training and development in this area to help him provide comprehensive services to the student.
d. Mr. Golden should terminate the counseling relationship with the student, as his beliefs are constitutionally protected.

27. A student who has been diagnosed with ADHD is demonstrating difficulty on standardized reading assessments due to her disability. Her school counselor is working with the Section 504 team to develop a plan for the student, including testing accommodations. Which of the following would NOT be an appropriate accommodation in this scenario?

a. Providing extended time to complete assessments
b. Having a test administrator read the assessments aloud
c. Providing frequent breaks during assessments
d. Eliminating the use of bubble sheets during assessments

28. Anne Roe's personality theory of career choice is based on the assumption that career choices are made to help satisfy a need shaped by:

a. Cultural contexts
b. Emotional factors
c. Valence and expectancies
d. Early childhood experiences

29. A seven-year-old student is engaged in a classroom guidance session focused on friendship skills. The student comments that "It is important to take turns, otherwise you will get in trouble with the teacher." This student's comment best aligns with which stage of moral development, according to Lawrence Kohlberg?

a. Obedience and punishment (stage 1)
b. Maintaining personal relationships (stage 3)
c. Law and order (stage 4)
d. Social contract (stage 5)

30. Which of the following is true regarding the rights of students and parents?

a. A counselor's primary obligation is to protect the student's right to confidentiality, but this right must be balanced with the parent's right to make decisions on their child's behalf.
b. A counselor's primary obligation is to protect the student's right to confidentiality, even if that is at odds with a parent's right to make decisions on their child's behalf.
c. A counselor's obligation to protect the student's right to confidentiality and the parent's right to make decisions on their child's behalf are equal.
d. A counselor's primary obligation is to protect the parent's right to make decisions on their child's behalf, as minor children do not have the right to confidentiality.

Refer to the following for question 31:

> Anthony is a 5th-grade student who struggles with focus and attention in the classroom. He has been getting poor grades on assessments and classwork for several months, complaining of headaches, and demonstrating a short attention span in class. His teacher has come to the counselor because she doesn't know how to help Anthony. He does not have a formal diagnosis of ADHD.

31. Which of the following would be an appropriate first step for the counselor to take in supporting Anthony?

a. The counselor should provide individual counseling to Anthony to improve his focus and attention.
b. The counselor should contact Anthony's parents to have them submit a written request for a special education evaluation.
c. The counselor should help the teacher identify areas of concern and work with the teacher to address those areas according to the school's intervention process.
d. The counselor should refer Anthony to the appropriate team for a special education evaluation.

32. An individual has begun to compare their accomplishments to those of their peers and feels a sense of pride in how they compare to others. According to Erik Erikson, this individual is in which stage of development?

a. Autonomy vs. shame (ages 2–3)
b. Initiative vs. guilt (ages 3–6)
c. Industry vs. inferiority (ages 6–12)
d. Identity vs. role confusion (ages 12–18)

33. A patient waits for their scheduled sleep study to address recurrent and persistent daytime napping and lapses into sleep. While in the waiting area, the patient laughs and jokes with another patient. This is followed by a sudden loss of muscle tone in the patient's neck and jaw. A likely diagnosis would be:

a. Hypersomnolence disorder
b. Insomnia disorder
c. Restless leg syndrome
d. Narcolepsy

Refer to the following for question 34:

A school counselor leading a counseling group for students whose parents are going through a separation or divorce generally sits and listens to the group's conversations but does not participate in the conversations or provide direction to the group.

34. All of the following accurately reflects the impact of divorce on families EXCEPT:

a. Rates of academic difficulties are higher for children of divorce.
b. Rates of emotional difficulties are higher for children of divorce.
c. Among children of divorce, boys have higher rates of maladjustment than girls.
d. Among divorced couples, divorced men report higher levels of life satisfaction than divorced women.

35. How did Albert Ellis view "self-talk" in his theory?

a. As the source of our emotional disturbances
b. As the symptom of neurosis or even psychosis
c. As a therapeutic technique for solving problems
d. As a kind of mental chatter that is to be ignored

36. A counselor from a small town begins working at an urban school. What action should the counselor take to ensure that she is aware of the difference in cultures between herself and her students?

a. Refer those students of differing cultures to another counselor. Since their cultures are different, she will not be able to help them.
b. Educate herself on the diversity of the school and the community.
c. Counsel the students with the confidence that she can help them no matter what.
d. Offer cultural diversity programs so that students can learn about each other.

Refer to the following for question 37:

> At the beginning of a counseling relationship, the counselor informs the student of confidentiality, stating that he cannot reveal anything that is discussed during the sessions no matter what. After a few sessions, the counselor feels that the student would benefit from extra sessions and offers to meet the student outside of school to talk over coffee. During these after-school sessions, the student informs the counselor that she is considering suicide. Since the counselor does not think this student will follow through, he disregards the statement.

37. What exception relating to confidentiality did the counselor neglect to discuss with the student?

a. Pregnancy
b. Harm to self or others
c. Sexual relationships
d. Problems with self-esteem

38. What issues might a primary prevention group address for adolescent girls?

a. Grief and loss
b. Aggressive behaviors
c. Self-esteem
d. Abuse

39. A school counselor who is leading a group counseling session wishes to stop a group member from monopolizing the conversation and allow others more floor time to participate. Which skill would the counselor utilize to accomplish this goal?

a. Summarizing
b. Blocking
c. Linking
d. Active listening

40. Which of the following is NOT an example of a criterion-referenced assessment?

a. End-of-grade exams
b. End-of-unit assessments
c. AP exams
d. The SAT

41. Which of the following types of assessments is best used to measure a student's mastery of concepts taught in a specific course?

a. Formative assessment
b. Diagnostic assessment
c. Summative assessment
d. Norm-referenced assessment

42. What is the difference between "undecided" and "indecisive" in terms of career counseling?

a. There is no difference; they are simply synonyms
b. An undecided individual needs more information
c. The indecisive individual needs more information
d. An undecided person always has trouble deciding

43. A middle school counselor is planning classroom guidance lessons about career options. Which of the following would be the best use of technology in order to increase student knowledge of various careers?

a. Using a survey platform to gather pre-lesson data about careers that interest students
b. Having students utilize a search engine to research a career of interest
c. Having students create a presentation about a career of interest
d. Using a career search such as O*NET to connect careers to skills and interests

44. A teen client (who is usually quite slovenly), tells his counselor that he's willing to shower, comb his hair, and dress well on Friday nights because it gains him the attention of a girl he likes. What operant conditioning principle is at work here?

a. Self-instructional principle
b. Token economy principle
c. Premack principle
d. Self-efficacy principle

45. Compared with high school students who enter the workforce right after graduation, students who go to college can expect to:

a. be hired at lower wages.
b. earn about $10,000 more per year.
c. work longer hours.
d. be hired to fill more unskilled positions.

46. When dealing with middle school students, it is important for a counselor to understand the developmental relationship between industry and inferiority. This is an example of a theory of development based on the work of what psychologist?

a. Freud
b. Piaget
c. Erikson
d. Bandura

47. Jake, a middle school student, makes a comment in class that he wishes he was "never born." The teacher refers Jake to the counselor based on his comment. What is the appropriate response for the school counselor in this scenario?

a. Call the crisis response number for a mental health evaluation.
b. Talk with Jake about making inappropriate comments in class.
c. Talk with Jake about his comments, and call his parents to let them know what he said.
d. Conduct a suicide screening, and determine the severity of Jake's threat.

48. A school counselor is leading a counseling group focused on developing study skills. During a particular session, the counselor encourages self-disclosure and points out similarities between group members. What is the counselor's goal in these types of comments?

a. Allaying anxiety
b. Establishing cohesion
c. Protecting the welfare of the individual
d. Establishing trust

49. A 16-year-old female with an intellectual disability reports chewing up her food, regurgitating it, and then rechewing it, reswallowing it, or spitting it out. Her symptoms are likely to meet the diagnostic criteria for:

a. Bulimia nervosa
b. Pica
c. Binge eating disorder
d. Rumination disorder

50. In designing and implementing a comprehensive school counseling program, which of the following is NOT a type of action plan utilized by the ASCA National Model?

a. Curriculum action plan
b. Small-group action plan
c. Closing-the-gap action plan
d. Use-of-time action plan

51. For which of the following group types do members experience transitions only after there are vacancies or a group member leaves?

a. Ongoing groups with a fixed membership
b. Time-limited groups with a fixed membership
c. Ongoing groups with revolving membership
d. Time-limited groups with revolving membership

52. In peer mediation programs, students are trained to guide peers through a conflict resolution process based on which of the following conflict resolution styles?

a. Competing
b. Collaborating
c. Avoiding
d. Accommodating

53. Which of the following statements is NOT true regarding academic outcomes for students from low-SES backgrounds?

a. Students from low-SES backgrounds typically have less access to college information than their middle- or high-SES peers.
b. The high school graduation rate is lower among low-SES students than middle- or high-SES students.
c. Students from low-SES backgrounds typically have lower reading and language skills than their middle- or high-SES peers.
d. The academic achievement of students from low-SES backgrounds is more affected by their home and family conditions than their school conditions.

54. In which of the following scenarios might a personality assessment, such as the Myers-Briggs Type Indicator (MBTI), be an appropriate tool?

a. Determining placement in honors coursework
b. Evaluating students for special education services
c. Identifying careers that may be of interest
d. Diagnosing an individual with a personality disorder

55. One major risk factor for students is having parents with little or no education or parents who do not speak English as a first language. As a counselor, how could you address this issue?

a. Offer educational opportunities for parents, such as reading and writing classes.
b. Suggest to parents that they enroll in college and earn degrees.
c. Develop educational programs that teach students to be independent of their families.
d. Provide counseling services to all students who have uneducated parents.

56. Which of the following resources would best be used to help a school counselor complete the use-of-time assessment?

a. The school district's student information system
b. Data collected from an online survey
c. A digital calendar, such as Google Calendar
d. Documentation of the counselor's sick leave

57. Which of the following scenarios is in violation of the Family Educational Rights and Privacy Act (FERPA)?

a. A 16-year-old student asks to view their educational record and is permitted to do so without parental consent.
b. A non-custodial parent asks to inspect their child's educational record and is permitted to do so without the custodial parent's consent.
c. A parent asks to review their child's educational record and then requests an item that they believe to be inaccurate be removed from the record.
d. A school creates a directory of student contact information and allows parents a 30-day notice to opt out of the directory.

58. Most approaches to career choice today are based on which theory?

a. Psychological
b. Trait-factor
c. Developmental
d. Social learning

59. A counselor is reviewing a client's record and discovers an inaccuracy. Unless otherwise dictated by agency or institutional policy, the counselor should:

a. Destroy and replace the original document.
b. Add a clinical note explaining the inaccuracy.
c. Explain the inaccuracies to the client and obtain permission to destroy the documentation.
d. Seek consultation and have the consultant document any necessary changes.

60. Which of the following statements is true regarding electronic communications according to the ASCA Ethical Standards for School Counselors?

a. Electronic communication between the school counselor and other individuals represents a form of privileged communication and is confidential.
b. Electronic communication between school officials about an individual student can create an official school record under FERPA.
c. Electronic communication about an individual student does not create an official school record under FERPA as long as the student's name is not used.
d. The only form of electronic communication that constitutes an official school record is that which takes place within the official student information system (SIS).

61. Mr. Garner is a school counselor who was asked to participate in an IEP meeting for one of his students. Which of the following best describes the role most appropriate for Mr. Garner in the IEP development process?

a. Mr. Garner should assess the student for special education eligibility and provide data regarding his assessments to the team.
b. Mr. Garner should determine if the child qualifies for an IEP under IDEA and, if so, which category the child qualifies under.
c. Mr. Garner should not participate in the IEP meeting because it is an inappropriate role for a school counselor.
d. Mr. Garner should advocate for the needs of his student and collaborate with the team to ensure the plan is appropriate.

62. Ms. Clark is a counselor who is working with a group of 9th-grade girls experiencing bullying. The four girls used to be friends, but for the last few months, three of the girls have been purposely leaving the fourth girl, Melissa, out of activities, including weekend parties and group work in class. They have also been spreading rumors about Melissa and telling other students not to be friends with her. Which type of bullying is taking place in this scenario?

a. Social bullying
b. Verbal bullying
c. Physical bullying
d. Cyberbullying

63. A child who behaves well to avoid punishment is in which stage of moral development?

a. Preoperational
b. Preconventional
c. Conventional
d. Concrete operational

64. Which of the following correctly matches the theorist with an adolescent's stage of development:

a. Piaget: concrete operational, Erikson: identity versus role confusion, Freud: phallic stage
b. Piaget: formal operational, Erikson: industry versus inferiority, Freud: genital stage
c. Piaget: formal operational, Erikson: identity versus role confusion, Freud: genital stage
d. Piaget: concrete operational, Erikson: industry versus inferiority, Freud: phallic stage

Refer to the following for question 65:

> A 5-year-old boy continues to attempt to play with children who openly ridicule him and leave him out of games. His persistence with this group of children has recently resulted in a number of fights on the playground. After being referred to your office, you learn that he has an unsupportive home life. His parents were divorced last year. He lives with his mother, who works at night, and he does not see his father. He is often left at home alone; however, a neighbor watches him from time to time.

65. According to cognitive behavior theory, what developmental skills is this child lacking?

a. Interpersonal skills
b. Abstract thinking skills
c. Concrete thinking skills
d. Self-identity

66. Which of the following is the most effective as a preventative, universal intervention for promoting communication and conflict resolution?

a. Primary prevention group
b. Structured intervention group
c. Individual counseling
d. Crisis counseling

67. A school counselor begins at a new school and notices that there are few cultural diversity programs available. What might she do to increase cultural expression in the school?

a. Ask teachers to provide information on the ethnic demographics of their classes.
b. Encourage families to discuss cultural diversity at home.
c. Coordinate a field trip to a more diverse school.
d. Develop programs and events that celebrate and educate students about cultural diversity.

68. Career construction theory is a narrative process used to integrate one's personality, experiences, and aspirations to create a:

a. Life theme
b. Life span
c. Life space
d. Life structure

69. A new counselor feels that it is necessary to help all students solve their problems as quickly as possible. Because of this, she routinely brings paperwork home. Why would this practice be frowned upon in the field of counseling?

a. Counselors are not paid to work at home.
b. Counselors should establish boundaries between their professional and personal lives.
c. Colleagues may become jealous because the counselor is more efficient than they are.
d. This practice could lead to dual relationships.

70. A high school counselor spends 20 minutes on the phone with a student's mental health therapist, discussing how school personnel can help to ensure the safety of the student after a recent mental health crisis. This is an example of which type of task?

a. Individual student planning
b. Responsive services
c. Consultation
d. Creating an action plan

71. Which of the following Neo-Freudian theorists most strongly believed that behavior can be understood best in terms of social interactions and interpersonal relationships?

a. Erich Fromm
b. Harry Stack Sullivan
c. Wilhelm Reich
d. Karen Horney

72. Cultural identity is:

a. Primarily influenced by race and ethnicity
b. Fully developed by early adulthood
c. Stable across changing contexts
d. Dynamic and constantly evolving

73. Ms. Martinez, a school counselor, receives a referral regarding a middle school student who was caught stealing food at school. Ms. Martinez meets with the student individually, and he tells her that he was hungry because he "doesn't get to eat at home" and "isn't allowed to eat when he is in trouble." Ms. Martinez also receives a report that, upon hearing of his disciplinary write-up, the student's sibling stated that he was lying about not being able to eat at home and that they both get plenty to eat. Which type of referral would be most appropriate for Ms. Martinez to make in this situation?

a. Ms. Martinez should refer the student to Child Protective Services due to suspicion of neglect, despite what the sibling stated.
b. Ms. Martinez should refer the student to child nutrition for an application for free lunch so that he doesn't get in trouble for taking food.
c. Ms. Martinez should refer the student to the principal, as this is a behavioral issue and not an issue of neglect.
d. Ms. Martinez should refer the student for additional individual counseling to address this behavior.

74. What is one reason a counselor might use an online college search with students?

a. To ensure students only apply to colleges for which they have a high chance of admission
b. To provide students with a wide knowledge base about various colleges
c. To eliminate the need for face-to-face individual student planning with the counselor
d. To ensure all students apply to colleges that they can afford without financial aid

75. What is the fourth stage of Jean Piaget's four stages of cognitive development?

a. Sensory Motor Stage
b. Preoperational
c. Concrete Operations
d. Formal Operations

Refer to the following for question 76:

> A counselor begins seeing a student who has issues with low self-esteem. This student is of Chinese descent but was adopted by an African American family as a baby. The counselor knows that children begin understanding their cultural identities by the time they are three years old.

76. What implication does this fact—that children begin understanding their cultural identities by the time they are three—have on the school counselor?

a. Counselors of a different culture should meet with parents to discuss their cultural beliefs before counseling a student.
b. This will not be an issue since cultural identity is already established by the time the child begins school.
c. This established identity must be respected and taken into consideration when addressing students' issues.
d. Cultural identity can be discounted in young children but must be addressed in older children.

77. Ms. McCoy is leading a counseling group for children whose parents are going through a divorce or separation. Which of the following would NOT be a goal of this type of support group?

a. Allowing children to share their feelings about their family situation
b. Allowing children to discuss the changes that are happening in their family
c. Allowing children to be reassured and feel hopeful about their situation
d. Allowing children to practice conflict resolution strategies and communication skills

78. Which of the following school counselor activities does NOT take place within the Manage component of the ASCA National Model?

a. Completing a use-of-time assessment
b. Analyzing a results report
c. Creating a closing-the-gap action plan
d. Writing a mission and vision statement

79. Which of the following school counselor roles is considered a direct service?

a. Consulting
b. Collaborating
c. Evaluating
d. Counseling

80. The sensorimotor period is part of whose developmental stage theory?

a. Freud
b. Piaget
c. Erikson
d. Kohlberg

Answer Key and Explanations for Test #2

1. D: Knowledge acquisition will occur throughout a person's life through formal education and life experiences; however, this is not considered a developmental task or milestone. Formation of a child's sense of identity is a developmental task that is developed in the early stages of life. Self-identity tells the child who they are and what that means to others. Delays or deficiencies in this process can lead to insecurities or confusion for a child. Autonomy, or the sense of independence, is typically developed during adolescence. This developmental milestone provides youth with a sense of purpose and self-ability. Finally, self-esteem is continuously developed throughout life. These developmental tasks are essential for a healthy emotional mindset.

2. C: The activities described would best apply to the working or norming stage of a small group. For this activity, students have already been selected and screened, established group norms, and begun the work of the group. They are working toward the goals established and learning the skills to help them there.

3. A: Thorough data analysis, including disaggregating data by subgroup, is typically used for either creating a closing-the-gap action plan or completing a school data profile. This type of data analysis is helpful for identifying potential achievement gaps or equity issues within the school or district that the counselor can plan to address with a closing-the-gap action plan. This type of detailed, schoolwide data analysis is typically not used for creating a small-group action plan, although a small group may be utilized as a strategy within a closing-the-gap action plan. The annual agreement is a document created between a counselor and an administrator to plan for and establish goals for the upcoming school year and is focused on the counseling program itself; a needs assessment is usually in the form of a survey completed by students, staff, and/or parents to identify strengths and areas of concern in the school.

4. A: A group setting in counseling can be very effective when a counselor takes time to develop positive group dynamics. During the group formation phase, participants are getting to know one another. Because of personal reasons, participants may be resistant to the group, be uncomfortable sharing, or not trust others in the group. It is important to focus the first session or sessions on developing guidelines for cooperation within the group. This process includes encouraging the participation of all group members and agreeing on group rules, goals, and objectives. A common technique during this stage is to allow group members themselves to develop their own rules, goals, and objectives. This activity encourages participation and gives the participants a sense of ownership and belonging within the group.

5. D: In this scenario, the student has progressed through school-wide and classroom-wide interventions, and targeted individual intervention is appropriate. A functional behavior assessment (FBA) is a detailed method of collecting data about a student's behavior in order to develop an appropriate plan for changing inappropriate behaviors. While anecdotal evidence and historical data can be helpful, the FBA will provide the most detailed information to create an effective plan.

6. B: Naturally, all of the answer choices are important to consider when administering pre-post tests. A counselor would not want to give a post-test designed for a first grader to kindergarten students. Also, an assessment for first graders is not likely to have 100 questions. However, during the development of this type of test, key ideas and concepts are important to consider. These key ideas and concepts will be the basis for all questions on the pre-post tests. This information must be related to the content being learned and be linked to state curriculum standards. These key ideas must also be grade appropriate. Pre-post tests will fail when this information is not appropriately presented.

7. D: Program evaluations are essential for guidance counseling programs. These evaluations will provide information on the effectiveness of a program and allow the counselor to make adjustments and improvements to these programs as necessary. When beginning an evaluation, the counselor should compile various forms of documentation about the program. This will include curriculum guides, unit lesson plans, and the school's master schedule for the counseling programs. This information will help give the counselor a picture of the school's current programs, which will allow the counselor to determine if the guidance curriculum is meeting the students' academic, emotional, and social needs.

8. A: Generally speaking, classroom guidance is a preventative activity; it is systematically delivered to all students. Intervention activities take place when an issue or problem is identified, therefore an activity that is systematically delivered to all students is not an intervention activity. Outreach involves "reaching out" of the school and into the community, and classroom guidance does not fit this description. While classroom guidance may be focused on academic topics, "academic" is not a type of counseling activity.

9. C: In this situation, the counselor needs more information before determining next steps. Talking to Sally privately will help the counselor determine what is happening and how to proceed.

10. A: Norm-referenced tests compare an individual's test score to those of a comparison group, typically a group of same-age or same-grade peers. For many state-standardized tests, a child's individual score is compared to a norm group of students across the state, and sometimes there are additional norm groups for the school or district. Parents who are trying to understand their child's test scores may confuse a percentile rank with a percentage of correct answers on the test itself, but they are very different data points. Norm-referenced tests compare an individual's performance to a comparison group, while criterion-referenced tests compare an individual's performance to a set of standards or objectives to be mastered. End-of-grade tests often do measure a student's mastery of grade-level standards, but the indication that this child's test score is from a "norm-referenced" test means that their results are calculated in comparison with their peers.

11. B: An educational group is one that is designed to teach information and develop skills, regardless of the topic. Therefore, a group that teaches parenting skills would be considered an educational group. A group that focuses on processing a common experience of grief and loss would be an example of a support group, while the group planning a school event would be a task group. Finally, the group focused on overcoming test anxiety would be considered a counseling or therapy group.

12. D: Only academic, career, and social/emotional domains are included in the ASCA Mindsets & Behaviors for Student Success. College readiness is a part of the Career domain; however, it is not the primary focus.

13. C: Linking is a strategy specifically for identifying "links" or commonalities between group members. Linking can help group members feel connected to one another and improve overall cohesion and interaction in the group.

14. B: The ASCA Mindsets & Behaviors for Student Success outlines skills and mindsets essential for student success in college and beyond. Counselors planning a classroom guidance curriculum should utilize the Mindsets & Behaviors to begin to outline learning objectives for their lessons.

15. D: There are a great number of factors that can be addressed to help students have a successful transition to middle school. Middle school represents a huge transition for many students, with academic, personal, social, and physical changes taking place very rapidly. There are several ways both elementary and middle school counselors can work to improve outcomes for new middle schoolers, including all of the topics addressed in answer choices A, B, and C. IEP specifics would not be discussed in this type of meeting because it would not be appropriate. Students' IEP teams hold special transition meetings to address the specific needs of individual students in transitioning to the next educational level.

16. C: A likely diagnosis would be ADHD. The child's behaviors consistent with ADHD include difficulties with staying on task, disorganization, and problems transitioning from one activity or setting to another. Children with ASD also display inattention but differ from those with ADHD in that the essential feature of ASD is impairments in reciprocal social interactions. Children with ODD exhibit behaviors required for complying with directives, hostility, angry or irritable mood, and vindictiveness. Children with conduct disorder commit serious violations of rules (e.g., running away, truancy), as well as aggression to animals, theft, and destruction of property.

17. D: A school counselor's skills in individual and small group counseling can certainly be a benefit to students with disabilities. However, as with all students, providing long-term individual counseling is out of the scope of appropriate responsibilities. By providing long-term individual counseling for students with IEPs, the counselor would be working outside of the scope of their training and expertise. In addition, providing this type of service to students with IEPs could lead to the school counselor only having time to provide IEP services, leaving general education students without access to the school counseling program.

18. C: Closing-the-gap action plan documents are used to develop plans to address discrepancies between groups of students. In the situation described, there appears to be a discrepancy between students with disabilities and nondisabled students in the rate of high school graduation, so a closing-the-gap action plan would be appropriate. Within that plan, a counselor may identify activities for classroom guidance lessons or small group counseling, but the overall plan to address the discrepancy is the closing-the-gap action plan. In addition, the documentation of activities and evaluation methods takes place within the closing-the-gap action plan template.

19. B: A business owner is the occupation that would give the client the highest job satisfaction. The client's code is ESC (enterprising, social, conventional). John Holland conceptualized six occupational and personality categories: realistic (R), investigative (I), artistic (A), social (S), enterprising (E), and conventional (C), or RIASEC. Holland used a hexagon to illustrate the positioning of each occupational category, with each point representing one of the Holland types. The SDS score is a three-letter code summarizing, in ranked order, the client's three dominant types. Enterprising careers include business owners. Biologists and lawyers are categorized as investigative. Interior decorators are categorized as artistic.

20. C: A school counselor should maintain confidentiality for their students, so seeking out information about community resources or mental health services utilized by students could pose a confidentiality issue. If agencies are utilized by other students that the counselor is aware of, the counselor should be careful to protect the privacy and confidentiality of those students in providing referral lists. To protect the counselor from liability, any referral lists should be vetted and approved by the school or district in accordance with district policy. It is always a good idea to contact individual agencies to find out if they are open and accepting new referrals, and to gather information about services provided and how to make a referral because the availability of these services can change very quickly.

21. A: Understanding the limits of confidentiality is a necessary part of informed consent, which should be established in the selection/screening process. Even though the expectations regarding confidentiality are addressed in the initial/forming stage of the group counseling process, the initial disclosure of the limits of those expectations should take place prior to the initial group session.

22. C: Making a gentle connection between group members is an appropriate strategy to draw out a quiet group member; this skill is known as "linking." Ignoring the fact that James is not participating in the group is not appropriate, as other group members may begin to focus on James's non-participation by trying to draw him out or by becoming withdrawn themselves. Pulling an individual group member aside during a group session is typically not appropriate, as it takes the focus away from the group's collective focus, and removing a member from the group can shake the trust of the remaining group members.

23. B: Trauma-informed practices would be the most reasonable place for this counselor to start when working with this family. The children experienced a traumatic event and are demonstrating classic effects of trauma. Family systems therapy would be conducted in a mental health setting with a trained therapist. Multi-tiered systems of support and positive behavior intervention and support may be somewhat helpful for the children, but trauma-informed practices are the best support for recovery from a traumatic experience.

24. B: Edgar Schein used the term career anchor to explain an individual's perception of their own values, skills, abilities, and interests in regard to work. Schein's eight career anchors include technical competence, general managerial competence, autonomy/independence, security/stability, entrepreneurial, service/dedication to a cause, challenge, and lifestyle. Active adjustment is a concept in the theory of work adjustment. Active adjustment refers to an employee's effort to change jobs or occupations if one's ability is not reflected in their current role. Career congruence, a concept developed by John Holland, describes the positioning of career types on a hexagon. Careers that are congruent are similar and are located near one another. Finally, life role salience is defined by Donald Super as the importance or meaning given to one's career and life role, including roles in which an individual derives the most meaning.

25. D: MST is an evidence-based practice (EBP) for adolescent substance abuse and associated issues. MST addresses severe behavioral issues, including community influences, school issues, and family factors. Family involvement is a critical element for adolescent substance use disorder treatment. The Incredible Years is an early childhood EBP for children with challenging behaviors, including symptoms of ADHD and ODD. The parent-implemented intervention is an EBP for children with ASD. Finally, self-help groups, including Alcoholics Anonymous and Narcotics Anonymous, are not EBPs for adolescent substance use and antisocial behaviors.

26. C: According to the ASCA Ethical Standards for School Counselors, counselors should evaluate any personal biases that may prevent them from providing comprehensive services to all students. When school counselors identify biases that interfere with providing comprehensive services to all students, they should seek additional training and development rather than deny counseling services to these students based on their personal biases. School counselors should work to promote an environment that respects diversity.

27. B: Students with disabilities frequently require accommodations or modifications during standardized testing in order to allow the student to demonstrate their knowledge effectively and reduce the impact of their disability on the assessment results. With standardized tests, however, it is also important for the test administration to be as consistent as possible among students so that the test results are reliable and valid. The student specifically is struggling with reading assessments, so having the test read aloud would not be an appropriate modification because that affects the validity of the test (reading the test aloud makes it a listening test, not a reading test). Each of the other accommodations listed would generally be appropriate as a testing accommodation for students with attention difficulties.

28. D: Anne Roe's personality theory of career choice is based on the assumption that career choices are made to help satisfy a need shaped by early childhood experiences. Sunny Hansen developed the integrative life planning concept of career development, which emphasizes the influence of cultural contexts, including gender, race, ethnic origin, and socioeconomic background. Eli Ginzberg viewed occupational choice as a process involving emotional factors, individual values, education, and the impact of reality. Victor Harold Vroom's expectancy model used the terms valance and expectancies. Vroom believed that career choice results from forces toward or away from decisions. Force is created by the interaction of valence (i.e., preferences) and expectancies (i.e., anticipated outcomes).

29. A: A focus on external punishment or consequences rather than concepts of morality is typical of seven-year-old children and is described by Kohlberg's "obedience and punishment" stage of development. The child's comment indicates the desire to avoid punishment as the main motivator for moral behavior. According to Kohlberg, most children under the age of nine are in stage 1 or stage 2 of moral development.

30. A: According to the ASCA Ethical Standards for School Counselors, a counselor's primary obligation is to protect the student's right to confidentiality. The Ethical Standards indicate that the counselor should balance this right with an understanding of the rights of parents to be "the guiding voice in their children's lives." Particularly when there is a risk of serious and foreseeable harm to the student, a student's right to confidentiality may need to be breached to prevent such harm and protect the rights of the parents.

31. C: Schools have various subtleties and names for the process of designing interventions for students, however, almost all schools have some type of formal intervention process. This may be called a multitiered system of supports (MTSS), response to intervention (RTI), student support team (SST), or a number of other names. Ultimately, the fundamental process is the same: Identify areas of concern and develop interventions to address those areas, then reassess after a specified amount of time to determine if progress is being made. While interventions such as individual counseling may be appropriate, the counselor and teacher would first need to identify specific areas of concern and determine if that intervention would be appropriate for Anthony. Typically, referrals for special education evaluations could occur as part of this intervention process, but they are almost never the first step to be taken.

32. C: In the industry vs. inferiority stage of development, an individual begins to compare their personal accomplishments (academic, relational, athletic, etc.) to their peers. As a result, they develop either a sense of pride or a sense of inferiority in comparison to others. The autonomy vs. shame stage focuses on developing the senses of independence and autonomy in a child who is given the opportunity to make basic decisions about their life, or a sense of shame when the child is not given such opportunity. In the initiative vs. guilt stage, a child learns a sense of pride when allowed to work toward a goal and practice responsibility, or a sense of guilt when they are unsuccessful in this task. Identity vs. role confusion is the stage in which adolescents grapple with the question "Who am I?"

33. D: A likely diagnosis for the patient is narcolepsy. Narcolepsy is a sleep-wake disorder characterized by frequent daytime napping or lapses in sleep. The DSM-5-TR includes cataplexy as a criterion for narcolepsy, which is defined as the sudden bilateral loss of muscle tone with maintained consciousness, generally preceded by laughter or joking. Narcolepsy is the only sleep-wake disorder that includes a specifier of cataplexy. Hypersomnolence disorder is characterized by excessive sleepiness despite getting at least 7 hours of sleep. Feeling unrested after long periods of time also occurs with hypersomnolence. Insomnia disorder is characterized by difficulty falling asleep, middle-of-the-night awakenings, and early rising without being able to go back to sleep. Finally, restless leg syndrome occurs when uncomfortable sensations precipitate the urge to move the legs during rest or inactivity.

34. D: Among divorced couples, divorced women report higher levels of life satisfaction than divorced men. For children of divorce, rates of academic and emotional difficulties are higher than those of children with married parents. Additionally, among children of divorce, boys are found to have higher rates of maladjustment than girls.

35. A: In his rational emotive behavior therapy (REBT) theory, Ellis stated that irrational belief systems, self-talk, and crooked thinking cause emotional disturbance and inappropriate affects and behaviors. While Ellis believed that self-talk is the source of emotional disturbance, it is not necessarily a symptom of neurosis or psychosis; Ellis was a cognitive-behavioral psychologist who had earlier subscribed to Freudian psychoanalysis but came to reject it by the early 1950s. In Ellis' paradigm, self-talk is not a problem-solving technique but a problem itself. While self-talk might be considered a kind of mental chatter, Ellis did not teach that it should be ignored, but rather that one should actively work to change irrational beliefs and behaviors through rational analysis and cognitive reconstruction.

36. B: While there may be times when a counselor may need to refer a student to a different counselor, this is not an effective alternative to a lack of cultural diversity education. When offering programs for cultural diversity education within the school, the counselor must have education in this area in order to create effective programs. Therefore, counselor education is the best way to ensure that students' needs are met. Most counselor training programs today offer multicultural training and education. Additionally, there are many opportunities for continued education in this area.

37. B: Although counselors have a responsibility to their clients, they are also ethically accountable for the safety of others; this must be disclosed at the beginning of a counseling relationship. If a client ever threatens to harm themselves or someone or something else, the rules of confidentiality do not apply. It is up to the counselor to make a professional judgment about any threatening statements a client might make to determine if alerting authorities and breaking confidentiality is necessary. Many counselors will consult with another professional if a situation is ambiguous. After determining the validity of a threat to do harm, counselors must inform their clients of their intent to notify the proper authorities.

38. C: Primary prevention groups aim at providing education and preventative counseling for a variety of problems. This type of group is beneficial for students who may have risk factors for future issues. These groups should focus on developing healthy lifestyles and center on the student's social, emotional, and cognitive abilities. Typically, a primary prevention group will discuss issues such as self-esteem, self-concept, listening skills, academic achievement, and methods of effective communication. Issues such as grief and loss, aggressive behaviors, and abuse are more often the focus of a problem-centered, structured intervention-counseling group. School counselors may conduct this type of group with students who have recently experienced a loss, have repeatedly violated school rules for fighting, or are known to have an abusive relationship.

39. B: Group leaders use blocking to stop (or "block") inappropriate or harmful behavior within the group. In this scenario, the counselor may use blocking to prevent the group member from monopolizing the conversation and then redirect the discussion to another group member.

40. D: Criterion-referenced assessments measure the test-taker's mastery of specific skills or objectives; results can typically be expressed in terms such as "passing" or "proficient." Students taking criterion-referenced assessments have either mastered the objectives or not; the abilities of other students taking the assessment have no impact on their score or test result. Norm-referenced assessments, however, compare the individual test-taker to their peers. These results are typically expressed as a percentile rank, rather than "passing" or "proficient."

41. C: A summative assessment is designed to be given at the conclusion of a unit of study, course, or grade level to measure learning outcomes and mastery of content standards. A summative assessment compares an individual's performance to the standards expected to be taught during the period being tested. A formative assessment is an assessment that is given during the unit of study, course, or grade level to monitor student learning and provide feedback to the instructor in order to adjust, reteach, or modify instruction going forward. A diagnostic assessment is typically given at the start of a unit of study, course, or grade level to determine the individual's prior knowledge or current level of performance in order to guide instruction, identify areas of need, or provide a benchmark for measuring growth when compared to a summative assessment. A norm-referenced assessment compares an individual's performance to a group of peers rather than to a set of standards or objectives to be mastered.

42. B: Undecided means that the person needs more information before making a decision; it refers to a state of being. Being indecisive, by contrast, is a personality trait. An indecisive person may be given all the information there is on a subject and may still be unable to decide. With indecisive clients, personal counseling may be needed before career counseling can be effective. Answer A is untrue since undecided and indecisive are not synonyms. Answers C and D are opposites of the correct definitions.

43. D: There are a variety of ways in which a school counselor can incorporate technology into classroom guidance lessons. When making choices about technology use in classroom guidance, it is important to consider the objective of the lesson and how technology supports the objective. In this scenario, the goal was to help students learn about various careers, so a career search engine such as O*NET would provide a wide variety of information and help students discover careers they may not have previously known about. The other answer choices only help students in reference to the careers they already have knowledge of or interest in, so they do not support the objective of "increasing student knowledge of various careers."

44. C: Premack's Principle of reinforcement was developed by David Premack in 1965 out of a study completed with monkeys. It states that high-probability behaviors (HPB) will reinforce low-probability behaviors (LPB). In the case of this question, the client doesn't like to shower and dress well. However, he is willing to do so because of the attention it gives him from a girl he likes. In other words, he is willing to engage in behavior he doesn't like in order to get something that he does. The Premack Principle has a variety of uses, included its use in animal training.

45. B: Individuals who go right into the workforce after high school graduation routinely earn substantially less than those individuals who go to college. Individuals who go to college would not be hired for unskilled positions, as they are overqualified. It would be hard to say whether or not the college-educated individuals would work longer hours than the non-college-educated individuals.

46. C: Erikson suggests that children begin to associate with either industry or inferiority in early adolescence. Industry refers to a person's ability to succeed and feel worthy. Typically, healthy children who receive the appropriate support and encouragement at home and at school will feel a sense of industry. This identification is important, as it can be the basis of future educational, social, and coping skills. For example, a child who has a strong sense of industry will be more likely to cope with a low grade on a test. They will understand that they may need to study harder for the next test or seek assistance. On the other hand, a child with a poor school, family, or peer support system may experience feelings of inferiority. In this case, they are likely to have insufficient coping mechanisms and not perform well in school.

47. C: The ASCA Ethical Standards for School Counselors indicate that counselors should use caution in reporting "serious and foreseeable harm." Even if the risk appears to be very low, counselors should always report threats or comments about self-harm to the students' parents. School counselors should refrain from conducting assessments for which they are not adequately trained and from making definitive statements regarding a student's risk level.

48. B: In this scenario, the counselor is focused on establishing group cohesion, or relationships among group members. Group cohesion is an essential trait for a successful counseling group, as group members begin to focus on the work of solving their collective problems.

49. D: Rumination disorder is characterized by repeated regurgitation of food for at least 1 month. Individuals with rumination disorder engage in rechewing, reswallowing, and spitting their food out. Infants and older individuals with intellectual disabilities are more likely to be diagnosed with rumination disorder. Individuals with bulimia nervosa discreetly consume amounts of food that are larger than most individuals would eat in the same time period. This is followed by inappropriate compensatory behaviors (e.g., excessive exercise, self-induced vomiting, refusing to eat, or misusing diuretics). Individuals with pica ingest nonnutritive substances (e.g., paint, plaster, or clay). Finally, binge eating disorder includes recurrent episodes of binge eating, eating until uncomfortably full, or socially isolating when eating.

50. D: The use-of-time assessment is an ASCA National Model document, but it is not an action plan. The use-of-time assessment analyzes the counselor's activities over the course of the school year and is typically done twice per year; as an assessment, it is a look backward over activities already conducted rather than a data-driven plan for future actions. Curriculum action plans, small-group action plans, and closing-the-gap action plans are all data-driven planning documents that help the counselor design interventions for the future. The curriculum action plan helps counselors create an effective plan for implementing the school counseling curriculum, and the small-group action plan is a similar document for planning small-group interventions. Closing-the-gap action plans help counselors design interventions focused on addressing discrepancies in academic or behavioral outcome data between student groups.

51. A: Members of ongoing groups with a fixed membership experience transition only after there are vacancies or when group members leave. Groups that are ongoing do not have an end date. In contrast, groups that are time limited have a set number of sessions. Membership can either be revolving or fixed, with revolving groups admitting new members when they become ready, and fixed groups beginning and ending with the same members unless a vacancy occurs, in which a new member may be added. Interpersonal process groups are generally ongoing with a fixed membership. Psychoeducational groups tend to be time limited with a fixed membership. Inpatient milieu therapy groups are considered ongoing groups with a revolving membership. Finally, art therapy (e.g., expressive) groups are an example of time-limited groups with revolving membership.

52. B: Peer mediation programs train student mediators to guide their peers through a collaborative conflict resolution process. Described as a "win-win" style, this conflict resolution style attempts to find a common solution that both parties can agree on. Other styles of conflict resolution may result in both parties not agreeing on the outcome. The competing style forces one member of the conflict to "win" at the expense of others, while the accommodating style sees one member of the conflict give in to the needs of the other member over their own. The avoiding style is exactly what it sounds like, and the conflict is ignored or postponed rather than addressed.

53. D: There are multiple factors that affect a student's educational outcomes, and students from low-socioeconomic status (SES) households are deeply affected by their circumstances. Numerous studies demonstrate the links between low-SES backgrounds and a variety of outcomes, including poor academic outcomes, lower graduation rates, inadequate literacy skills, and lower rates of college enrollment. While the home circumstances of a low-SES student affect their academic outcomes, the school environment of low-SES students is a stronger predictor of academic outcomes. Schools in low-SES communities are less likely to have highly qualified teachers with years of experience and high-quality training, as well as access to libraries and computers. All of these factors impact the academic outcomes for students in these communities, possibly even more than their home and family circumstances.

54. C: Personality assessments, such as the Myers-Briggs Type Indicator, can be useful tools for a variety of purposes, including self-reflection, learning coping skills, and identifying areas of academic or career interest. They are not, however, diagnostic assessments to be used for diagnosing personality disorders, evaluating for learning disabilities, or determining placement in special education or honors coursework. Personality assessments like the MBTI require an individual to be able to accurately reflect on and interpret their own thoughts, feelings, and behaviors and rate them accurately, and therefore should never be utilized as a sole data point in decision-making.

55. A: As communities become more diverse, counselors are seeing an increase in the number of parents who do not speak English as a first language. Because this dynamic often creates a barrier between these parents and their children's schools, a lack of participation from these parents is common. In these cases, counselors can provide information or opportunities for parents to increase their English skills through free or low-cost programs. Additionally, adult education programs in basic reading, writing, and GED preparation can be offered to parents who wish to increase their skills or earn their GED. Educated parents are able to offer more academic assistance to their children.

56. C: The use-of-time assessment is a document that helps school counselors determine how much of their time is spent in each of the components of the ASCA National Model, including the breakdown of direct and indirect services. The ideal breakdown of time is 80% spent on direct and indirect student services, while the remaining 20% goes to school support and program management. While many school counselors could estimate their use of time and enter that information into a survey or Excel spreadsheet, a calendar such as Google Calendar would be more likely to help counselors accurately calculate their use of time. The school's student information system may have helpful information about student use of time or fair-share duties, depending on how the school uses the program, but this would not be as useful as the digital calendar. Sick time documentation would not help counselors determine how they are using the time they are at school.

57. A: Under FERPA, students do not become "eligible students" who are granted access to their educational records until they are 18 years old or attending a post-secondary institution. Therefore, a 16-year-old would need their parents to request access to their records. Parents are permitted to inspect or request items be removed from their child's educational record at any time; even if the parent does not have physical custody of the child, they are permitted access to educational records unless a court order states otherwise. Schools are permitted to create a directory of student contact information as long as parents are given "reasonable time" to opt out of sharing directory information.

58. A: The psychological theory of career choice, developed by John Holland, is the basis for the vast majority of approaches to career choice today. Holland's theory, known as either a psychological or personality theory, focuses on the fit between an individual's personality type and their work environment or career choice. The trait-factor approach developed by Frank Parsons is not as popular today as it once was. Developmental theories (such as those developed by Donald Super, Eli Ginzberg, and associates) and social learning theories (such as those of John Krumboltz) may be of interest to school counselors who work with children, but are not as widely used or popular as Holland's theory.

59. B: The counselor should add a clinical note explaining the inaccuracy unless otherwise dictated by agency or institutional policy. The ACA Code of Ethics (2014) states, "Counselors take reasonable steps to ensure that documentation accurately reflects client progress and services provided. If amendments are made to records and documentation, counselors take steps to properly note the amendments according to agency or institutional policies." Destroying and replacing the original document or asking the client for permission to do so are unethical practices. Consultation may be sought; however, correcting the inaccuracy is ultimately the responsibility of the counselor.

60. B: Any form of electronic communication between the school counselor and other school officials can create an official school record that needs to be treated appropriately under FERPA, even if student names are not used. All forms of electronic communication should adhere to the ethical standards, and special care should be taken to protect confidentiality by utilizing accepted security standards. The ASCA Ethical Standards encourage counselors to take care in purging electronic sole-possession case notes, similar to hard-copy sole possession case notes.

61. D: According to ASCA, school counselors work with and advocate for the needs of students with special needs in a variety of ways, including being part of the IEP team. It is not appropriate for a counselor to lead the IEP team, coordinate special education, administer educational testing or assessments, or make sole determinations regarding IEP qualifications; however, it is appropriate for a school counselor to collaborate with the IEP team to advocate for the child's needs, ensure that the plan is appropriate, and help parents and students understand the plan.

62. A: The situation described is social bullying. Melissa is being excluded, and her relationships with friends and classmates are being damaged by rumors and exclusion. Social bullying is also called relational aggression. Verbal bullying includes name-calling, threats, mean comments, or jokes at the expense of another person. Physical bullying includes hitting, kicking, fighting, tripping, or other types of physical harm. Cyberbullying is bullying behavior that takes place online or through screens and can incorporate other types of bullying, such as social and verbal bullying.

63. B: Kohlberg's theory of moral development includes three levels and six stages. The first of which is the preconventional level. Children in stage 1 of the preconventional level obey rules to avoid punishment. Piaget's theory of cognitive development includes the preoperational stage, which is defined by egocentric thinking. Kohlberg's conventional level includes stage 3 (i.e., "good boy/good girl" orientation), and stage 4 (i.e., law and order orientation). Finally, Piaget's concrete operational stage is marked by the capacity for children to manipulate information to form mental operations.

64. C: The correct match for an adolescent's stage of development is Piaget: formal operational, Erikson: identity versus role confusion, Freud: genital stage. Piaget's concrete operational stage occurs between the ages of 7 and 11. Erikson's industry versus inferiority stage occurs in school-aged children or preteens. Finally, Freud's phallic stage of development occurs in children ages 3-6.

65. A: Interpersonal skills are the skills necessary to relate to and understand peer interactions. These skills begin developing at an early age and are reinforced by responses from others. Typically, a child with adequate interpersonal skills has the ability to understand if he is not liked or welcomed by his peers. This situation would result in the child's becoming withdrawn and possibly depressed. However, in this case, the child does not seem to possess this ability. While his interpersonal skills are so stunted that he does not recognize when he is not liked, there may be a deeper physiological explanation for his problems. It will be important for the counselor to gain as much information as possible from the family and others in contact with this child, and a referral to a specialist may be necessary.

66. A: Primary prevention groups are most effective for preventative, universal intervention. School counselors should be cognizant of the school environment. This awareness will allow the counselor to determine main areas in which students are struggling. A counselor who notices a lot of bickering and fighting in the hallways in between classes may decide that school-wide prevention groups are necessary. A school-wide prevention program in communication and conflict intervention will serve to educate the students about these basic skills. On the other hand, if the counselor provides only individual counseling or problem-centered counseling, the focus is likely to be on a specific problem rather than on education on how to avoid or resolve a conflict.

67. D: Education is the key to increasing tolerance and understanding between various cultures. Developing educational programs for students as well as teachers can offer a venue for these individuals to ask questions and gain a clear understanding of cultural diversity. It is also an opportunity to eliminate negative stereotypes. Additionally, offering programs or opportunities for students to celebrate their cultures will serve to provide education about other cultures to students from all backgrounds. These opportunities can be as simple as announcing various holidays celebrated by the different cultures in the school or allowing students to display pictures or information about their cultures in the halls of the school.

68. A: Career construction theory is a narrative process used to integrate one's personality, experiences, and aspirations to create a life theme. Mark Savickas' career construction theory asserts that individuals construct careers through meaning-making, which comprises an amalgam of memories, experiences, and personality traits. Life span and life space are associated with Donald Super's theory of career development. Super maintained that there were three aspects of career development, including life span, life space, and self-concept, each incorporating personal and situational factors. Life salience is the level of importance people attach to the various roles they play. The importance or meaning attached to each role makes up what Super calls one's life structure.

69. B: Counselors must establish boundaries between their professional and personal lives. It is a very common characteristic in this field for a counselor to want to help or fix all students in need. However, this is not practical and will eventually cause counselors to experience burnout. Counselors can avoid this by managing their work time properly and not taking work home. Additionally, counselors should schedule short breaks throughout the day where they can focus on something not related to counseling. These professionals should have down time every day and try to spend quality time with their friends and family when not at work.

70. C: Consultation is an indirect service conducted on behalf of the student for the student's benefit, while individual student planning and responsive services are both examples of direct services provided directly to the student. Creating an action plan is an ASCA National Model tool based on schoolwide or subgroup data that does not involve an individual student.

71. B: Harry Stack Sullivan favored a social systems approach to understanding human behavior. He felt that human behavior is best understood in terms of social interactions and interpersonal relationships. Erich Fromm believed that individuals could develop self-fulfillment, or social character, through joining with other people and could become lonely and unproductive if they did not. He felt that society offers opportunities to experience mutual love and respect. Wilhelm Reich contributed to the body therapy manipulation movement, and he believed that repeated successful orgasms were necessary for mental health. Karen Horney believed that security motivates every individual and a lack of security causes anxiety. She felt that irrational attempts to repair disrupted relationships could turn into neurotic needs.

72. D: Cultural identity is dynamic and constantly evolving. Cultural identity is multifaceted and is impacted by race, ethnicity, gender, religion, spirituality, socioeconomic status, profession, and sexual orientation. One's cultural identity is a social construct and continues to be formed through social interactions and is impacted by historical and political contexts.

73. A: School counselors are mandated reporters, and as such, they are required to report any cases in which they suspect abuse or neglect to the appropriate social service agency. Regardless of the student's sibling stating that abuse or neglect did not occur, the student's original statements provide a reason to suspect abuse or neglect. It is not the duty of the counselor to investigate and determine if abuse or neglect did in fact occur. Each of the additional answer choices may have an appropriate place in the next steps for the student, but in cases of suspected abuse or neglect, a referral to social services is always the first step.

74. B: Online college searches provide a wide knowledge base that could not be achieved with the counselor's knowledge alone. A counselor should utilize all college search tools appropriately to help students learn more about various colleges, not to encourage or discourage students from applying to specific colleges. School counselors provide students with the information and tools to make informed choices about college applications and admissions, but they should not impose their beliefs about specific colleges or plans on students. An online search tool cannot replace the goal setting and individual planning achieved in face-to-face planning with a school counselor.

75. D: Jean Piaget's last stage of development, formal operations, is when the individual's thinking becomes less tied to reality, and they are more able to use abstract reasoning and formal logic. When faced with a problem during this stage, the child is able to systematically solve problems in a more methodical manner. Jean Piaget theorized that cognitive development is tied to one's ability to process new information. Piaget's stages, in order, are sensory motor (involving motor skill and sensory input), preoperational (increased verbalizations and crudely formed concepts), concrete operations (organized thought and logic), and formal operations.

76. C: One crucial role of the school counselor is to assist students when they face problems. Counselors must be sensitive to students' needs, beliefs, and values, including their established cultural identity. A student's cultural identity will affect the way they learn and respond to counseling. Understanding cultural diversity and identity will also be important for counselors when developing working relationships with the student's parents. Those who are insensitive to cultural identity will find it difficult to gain student and parent trust and cooperation. In order to do this, school counselors must fully educate themselves on cultural diversity in general, as well as learning the specific demographics of the school they work in.

77. D: Skill practice is typically not a stated goal of a support group and would not be appropriate in this situation. Skill practice would be more appropriate for an educational or therapy group.

78. B: Analyzing a results report is part of the Assess component of the ASCA National Model, not the Manage component. Results reports are used to evaluate the effectiveness of classroom instruction, small-group services to students, and closing-the-gap action plans. Completing a use-of-time assessment, creating a closing-the-gap action plan, and writing a mission and vision statement are all part of the effective management of a comprehensive school counseling program. These activities help counselors clarify the needs of their school and students and define priorities for their program.

79. D: Counseling is a direct student service, while consulting, collaborating, and evaluating are all indirect services. Specifically, counseling is a responsive, direct service. Consultation and collaboration can be easily confused for direct services because they involve working directly with other professionals or stakeholders, often in "direct" response to a student need. However, direct services are defined as services provided to students.

80. B: Piaget's theory has the following stages: sensorimotor, preoperational, concrete operational, and formal operational (and later post-formal operations). Freud, Erikson and Kohlberg also have staged theories regarding human development, but none of them includes a stage named Sensorimotor.